Enjoy The story!

NOLAN RYAN
texas fastball to cooperstown

BY

KEN ANDERSON

Ken Anderson

EAKIN PRESS · Austin, Texas

FIRST EDITION
Copyright © 2000
By Ken Anderson
Published in the United States of America
By Eakin Press
A Division of Sunbelt Media, Inc.
P.O. Drawer 90159 ⌨ Austin, Texas 78709-0159
email: eakinpub@sig.net
💻 website: www.eakinpress.com 💻

1 2 3 4 5 6 7 8 9
Paper . . . ISBN 1-57168-349-6
Hardback . . . ISBN 1-57168-350-X

Library of Congress Cataloging-in-Publication Data

Anderson, Ken, 1949-
  Nolan Ryan: fastball to Cooperstown / by Ken Anderson; with an
introduction by Reid Ryan.
    p.   cm.
  Includes bibliography.
  Summary: A biography of Texas native Nolan Ryan, focusing on his
baseball career, from Little League to the majors.
    ISBN 1-57168-350-X (hbk.)   ISBN 1-57168-349-6 (pbk.)
  1. Ryan, Nolan, 1947—Juvenile literature. 2. Baseball players—
United States—Biography—Juvenile literature. [1. Ryan, Nolan, 1947-
2. Baseball players.]   I. Title.
GV865.R9 A63   1999
796.357'092—dc21
  [B]   99-042362

To my father —
who taught me to play catch and took me to my first
big league game at Forbes Field where we saw
Hall of Famer Roberto Clemente play.

Contents

What's It Like To Be Nolan Ryan's Son?

by Reid Ryan

It's like every American kid's dream come true.

I traveled all over the United States. Yankee Stadium, Fenway Park, Wrigley Field, Candlestick Park—these were my summer playgrounds. Kirby Puckett, Reggie Jackson, Rod Carew, Cal Ripkin, Jr., were more than names on baseball cards—they were people I knew.

One of my best memories happened during the 1986 League Championship Series between my dad's team, the Astros, and the New York Mets. I was the bat boy, which meant I wore a uniform, sat in the dugout, and helped the players. It was an exciting series. Dickie Thon hit a critical homer for us, and all the team ran onto the field to congratulate him. I got there first, and we traded high fives as he crossed the plate. That picture made the front page of the newspapers the next day.

When I was a junior in high school, I was taking

batting practice with my dad's team on a road trip to Minnesota. I hit a home run in the Metrodome! That same trip, the grounds crew took a liking to me and asked if I wanted to go up to the top of the dome to help make a repair. "Sure," I said. It's a long way up to the top of that inflatable dome. You can actually stand outside on the top of it and see all the buildings of downtown Minneapolis. You can also jump up and down while you're there. The grounds crew didn't really need to make a repair—they just wanted to let me jump around on the top. Imagine . . . using the Metrodome as a giant trampoline. It was a blast!

There were also some funny things. We were at Yankee Stadium one day. I was in uniform and was going to be warming up the outfielders. I lost track of the time. One of the players came running up to me with my glove and a baseball. He told me to hurry onto the field, that they were waiting for me. As I charged out into right field, I heard the umpire scream, "Time!" Too late for me, I realized the game had already begun. That incident made ESPN's "Sports Center" with a clever story about "Bat Boy Stops Game."

But having Nolan Ryan for a dad wasn't all fun and games. He was gone a lot. During my whole Little League and high school career he saw me play twice. He was never able to coach my team. As for playing sports, I was always in a no-win situation. If I did good in basketball or baseball it was because I was Nolan Ryan's son. If I didn't do well, people commented on that too.

But the good far outweighed the bad. I truly had a great childhood.

With this kind of upbringing, people often tell me, "It would be easy for you to be a real jerk." I always tell them, "My dad wouldn't let me." That's why my dad is such a hero to me. He never let my brother, sister, or me get "too big for our britches." He taught us that just because he played baseball didn't mean we were better than anyone else. He showed us what a blessing it was to have opportunities, and he taught us not to take those opportunities for granted. He passed on the values he and my mom learned growing up in a small town in Texas.

Whenever my dad has had questions in his life, he has looked toward the lessons his parents taught him as a kid—lessons of right and wrong. He has taught me how to be a man through his life both on and off the baseball field. Through his hard work and dedication to his job, his faith, and his family, he has passed on the same values his parents taught him. His story is one that every person can learn from. I know I still do.

My dad has taken the combination of experiences learned from his parents and the lessons he learned on the baseball field and has applied them to his life. My dad is a hero to people because he has led by example. On and off the field he has set goals and worked to attain them. Along the way he gave every person respect, no matter how famous he became.

As you read this book about my dad's life, you'll learn about his blazing fastball, his 5,000 strikeouts, his seven no-hitters and 300 wins. But these will not be his biggest contributions in life. Nolan Ryan will have positively affected more people's lives than all the hitters he faced combined over 27 years. That's what being a hero or legend is all about. And that's why when someone asks me, "What is it like to be Nolan Ryan's son?" I always respond, "It is every kid's dream."

Reid and his wife, Nicole, live in Round Rock, Texas, where Reid is president of the Round Rock Express, a double-A team in the Houston Astros' system. He hosts "Fishing and Hunting in Texas" on Fox Sports Southwest.

LITTLE LEAGUER

1947–1960

1

"Strike three!"

Those are the two words every pitcher loves to hear.

No big league pitcher ever heard those words more often than Nolan Ryan. By the time his major league career was over, he had struck out 5,714 batters. That's a record that most people think will never be broken.

Nolan's most famous pitch was his fastball. Of course, all major league pitchers are supposed to throw the ball fast, right? But no one ever threw it faster than Nolan. Some scientists once measured its speed at over 100 mph. That pitch made the Guinness Book of

World Records. *A major league umpire said that it seemed to "explode" when it got to the plate.*

Imagine if you were a batter. There on the pitcher's mound, just 60 feet 6 inches away, stands Nolan Ryan. All 6 foot 2 inches of him. He winds up, lifts his left knee all the way to his shoulder, and then releases a hardball with the speed of a train right to the plate. You have half a second before it goes thwap! into the catcher's mitt. Good luck.

Most hitters didn't have much luck against Nolan. Even Mark McGwire was struck out three times in one game by Nolan. In fact, name any great baseball hitter, from Hank Aaron to Ken Griffey, Jr., to Sammy Sosa—Nolan struck them all out.

By the time his playing days were over, Nolan set 53 major league pitching records. There was the career strikeout record of 5,714, the single-season record of 383 strike-outs, and the seven no-hitters. Put it all together—a total of 324 wins—and you can see why Nolan Ryan ended up in the Baseball Hall of Fame with the second highest percent-age of votes ever.

Today, if you drive south of Houston, Texas, you may be on a highway the state legislature named the Nolan Ryan Expressway. When you come to Nolan's

*hometown of Alvin, you'll see a big sign wel-
coming you to the "Hometown of Nolan Ryan
#34." The high school ballfield proclaims
"Nolan Ryan Field, Home of the
Yellowjackets." A life-size bronze statue of
him stands in front of city hall, and a building is named after him at Alvin Community
College.*

*But back in 1947, no one in Alvin had
ever heard of Nolan Ryan. He had been born
in another small Texas town, called Refugio,
just six weeks before his family moved to
Alvin . . .*

NOLAN RYAN WAS THE youngest of six kids. His dad,
Lynn Nolan Ryan, Sr., worked as a supervisor for an oil
company called Pan American. They wanted Mr. Ryan
to work at a refinery near Houston, so the Ryans had
to move. Nolan's mother, Martha, liked the always
green oak trees in Alvin. She also liked that the town
had good schools and was close enough to Mr. Ryan's
work. So Alvin was where they rented a house.

3

Many people might not think much of a town like Alvin. In those days only 5,000 people lived there. And it was hot. Texas summers can be brutal, and most people had no air conditioning back then. Plus, because it was just a short distance from the Gulf of Mexico, the air was always humid. Then there were the mosquitoes. Lots of them. Texas-size mosquitoes.

There you have it. Small town. Hot, humid, no air conditioning, plenty of mosquitoes. But for Nolan it was home. In fact, it was paradise.

Nolan grew up with four big sisters, Lynda, Mary Lou, Judy and Jean, and one big brother, Robert. Nolan's father would work long, hard hours, but he was home every night and on weekends. Mrs. Ryan, like most mothers of that time, stayed home. She cooked dinner, baked, cleaned, and made sure the family was taken care of. With six kids, there were few dull moments for Nolan.

Nolan was especially lucky to have a big brother. Robert was seven years older than Nolan, but when Nolan was old enough, he let him tag along.

Robert was a good athlete. He taught Nolan to catch in their backyard. Nolan would shag balls for Robert and his friends.

The kids cleared a vacant lot as their baseball field. Nolan spent hours on that field. The games ran all summer long. There really wasn't much else to do. Most moms sent their kids out to play. No one thought about watching TV during the day. In those days before cable, there wasn't anything for kids to watch anyway.

Everywhere that Nolan went, Suzy did too. Suzy was his brown and white fox terrier. From the time he was a little kid all the way through high school, when you saw Nolan, you usually saw Suzy.

One day Suzy saw a skunk. She chased it into a pile of brush. Nolan followed. Big mistake.

The skunk got away but left a very unpleasant odor on Suzy and Nolan. Mrs. Ryan wasn't happy, but she knew what to do. Nolan and Suzy took a bath. A bath of tomato juice. Many big cans of tomato juice. It wasn't an enjoyable bath, but it did the trick.

Nolan liked other animals too. One day he decided to buy a two-day-old calf. The little fella could fit into a feed bag. Nolan bottle fed it until it was big enough to sell.

He took the profit from that calf and bought two more. He decided raising calves was fun and profitable. He rented a pasture outside town and continued to raise calves until he went to high school. That rented pasture was his first ranch.

When Nolan wasn't playing baseball, he had lots of other things to do. He had his bike, which he could ride all over town. He was also a Cub Scout.

Nolan liked to throw things. Mustang Bayou, near

his house, was a great place to throw rocks at the water moccasins.

Nolan's first baseball cards cost one cent each (you also got a stick of bubble gum for that penny). As Nolan grew older the five-cent pack (five cards, one big flat piece of pink bubble gum) was popular. Those cards got a lot of use. Kids traded them, flipped them, and read the batting averages. The cards for less popular players ended up being attached with a clothes pin to the kids' bike wheels. They would make a noise as the spokes hit them that sounded just like a motor bike. Nolan loved to "motor" around Alvin with his spokes hitting the attached baseball cards.

While Nolan was enjoying as much freedom as a kid could have, he knew he had to be back home for dinner every night. Dinner was a time when all eight Ryans gathered around the table. Mrs. Ryan would prepare meat and potatoes every night. Mr. Ryan would say grace and the family would all talk about their days as they ate.

Mrs. Ryan was a good cook. Nolan especially liked his mother's fried chicken. His mother also made a dessert for each meal. Nolan's favorite dessert, chocolate pie, was reserved for special occasions.

The only bad part of dinners was the once a week beet night. Nolan hated beets. But the rule was that each kid had to eat two beets. Nolan ate his. After all, if you didn't eat your beets you weren't going to get dessert.

The Ryans' routine also included an active church

life. Every Sunday morning, the Ryans went to Sunday school and church at the local Methodist Church. Nolan even sang in the youth choir. When he grew older, he was involved in the Methodist Youth Fellowship activities. Church was followed by a big Sunday dinner.

There was only one real problem Nolan had growing up. School. It was awful.

Nolan was plenty smart. He just didn't learn like everyone else. He was dyslexic, which meant that he had a lot of trouble learning to read. He had trouble with writing and numbers too. To make matters worse, Nolan had a speech impediment.

The Alvin school didn't have any special programs for kids like Nolan. One of Nolan's teachers decided to flunk Nolan and make him repeat a grade. Mrs. Ryan talked the school into letting Nolan go to summer school instead.

Nothing really helped. School was going to be a real struggle for Nolan. For three summers—three hot Texas summers—Nolan had to sweat in an indoors classroom while the other kids were out playing.

But whatever problems he had in school with reading and stuttering made no difference on the playing field. Nolan was admired by his friends for being good at sports.

When Nolan was seven, his father took him to the

Alvin Hardware Store. The store had plenty of hardware, but it also had a sporting goods section with mostly hunting and fishing gear. There was a small selection of baseball gloves.

Since he was the youngest of six kids, Nolan never got anything new. Everything was a hand-me-down. But now his dad was letting him pick a brand new glove! There were a few Rawlings and Spalding brand gloves, but Nolan knew what he wanted. He wanted a Nocona. Young Nolan was a true Texan, and what could be better than a Nocona glove made in Nocona, Texas?

The glove became Nolan's prize possession. That night he slept with it. It lasted him quite a few years. He still has it.

The Ryans were a long way from poor. But with six kids, there weren't any luxuries and there was never any "extra" money. Nolan's parents, who hadn't gone past high school, were determined that all of their children were going to college. The problem was how to pay for it.

The answer to the college problem came when Nolan was in second grade. The *Houston Post* paper route for Alvin came open, and Mr. Ryan became the new distributor. That meant 1,500 papers had to be delivered every morning, seven days a week. Also, each customer had to be contacted each month to collect payment. All of this work was going to be in addition to Mr. Ryan's full-time refinery job.

Young Nolan was going to learn some very important lessons about hard work. His father wasn't just going to tell Nolan about it. Nolan was going to be part of the "team."

Every day Mr. Ryan, Robert, and Nolan got up at 1:00 A.M. They would drive down to an abandoned Sinclair gas station in downtown Alvin, where the papers had been left by the delivery truck. There they would roll the papers and tie them with a piece of string so they could be thrown from the car.

After enough papers were rolled, Mr. Ryan and Robert took off to deliver them. Nolan stayed behind and rolled the rest by himself. His dad and brother would return later for more. Nolan was really good at rolling papers. He could do 50 papers in about five minutes.

When he was done, he would go home and get back in bed. He was usually back home by 4:00 or 5:00 A.M.

In the mid-1950s, the Little League arrived in Alvin. The parents built a field, and kids were going to have their first chance at organized ball.

As a nine-year-old, Nolan was in the minor league. No matter to him. Baselines, umpires, coaches, a plate—this was the real thing. And Nolan was going to enjoy every bit of it.

The best part was the uniform. Nolan had a real

uniform—a flannel shirt and a real baseball cap. The boys wore the caps everywhere, even to school.

Most teams weren't named after major league teams as they frequently are now. They could be named after animals, colors, or just about anything. Nolan's first team was named after a law enforcement agency. They were the Rangers. No one could imagine then that nearly 40 years later, Nolan would end his baseball career playing for another team called the Rangers.

Nolan had fun in Little League. He was a good player but not great. There were other good players too.

When Nolan was 11 and 12 he made the All-Stars. He finally got a full uniform. The front of the jersey said "Alvin All-Stars."

As an All-Star, Nolan played out-of-town games. This was his first chance to play kids he didn't know. It was also a chance to see other towns.

The goal of every Little Leaguer was to go to the Little League World Series in Williamsport, Pennsylvania. The game wasn't televised then, but every kid knew about it. It just couldn't get any better than going to a game like that.

The Alvin All-Stars never came close to Williamsport. They were lucky to get as far as West Columbia, about 30 miles down the road.

One year, when they were eliminated from the All-Star tournament and their season was over, there was a closing ceremony. A man presented some awards and spoke to the kids. "One day, one of you Little Leaguers will go on to play in the major leagues."

10

Nolan would later describe that moment. It was "like a bell went off in my head. I became very excited." When he got home, he couldn't wait to tell his mother. "It's me that he meant, Mom! I'm sure it was me that he was talking about."

ALL-STATE PLAYER

NOLAN TURNED 14 in 1961. That was a big birthday for the eighth-grader. At 14, you could get a driver's license. Nolan was ready.

Nolan started looking for a car. He found a 1952 fire engine red Chevy sedan with two doors. It cost $50 and ran well. Perfect.

The Chevy changed his role on the family paper route. Now Nolan got up at 1:00 A.M., rolled some papers, and took off on the rural part of the route while his father did the town.

There was Nolan, out in the middle of the night, covering 50 miles with a car full of papers. He kept the window down, steered with his right hand, and flung the papers with his left hand.

High school was a happy time for Nolan. He still

struggled with his grades, but now he could play school sports. For Nolan, that was basketball and baseball.

Nolan thought he was better at basketball than baseball. He had grown to be 6 feet 2 inches tall. Although he was tall, he was not the tallest kid on the team. Still, Nolan could jump and was a good athlete. All through high school, Nolan played both basketball and baseball.

When Nolan was 15, he had his first date. The girl was named Ruth Holdorff. Since Nolan had a car, they could go to a movie and get a Coke at the Dairyland afterwards. Ruth became Nolan's girlfriend. She was the only girlfriend Nolan ever had.

Ruth was also athletic. In tenth grade Ruth won the state high school championship in tennis doubles. She liked baseball and basketball too.

By the time Nolan was in tenth grade, his fastball was really getting fast. But his pitches were awfully wild. He didn't have much of a curveball. There were at least two pitchers on his high school team that the coach thought were better than Nolan.

But something important was going to happen to Nolan—and to baseball—when he was in the tenth grade. He was going to meet Red Murff.

Red was a scout for the New York Mets. His job was to find the best pro prospects from high school and sign them for the Mets. Red was a real baseball man and knew his business well.

One Saturday morning in March, Red was driving from Galveston to Houston and had an extra hour. He decided to stop by Alvin High School. By luck, there was a game going on. When Red got his seat, it was the second or third inning. Alvin High was in trouble and the coach had just put in a new pitcher. The pitcher was a tall, skinny kid.

Red sat back and watched the new pitcher throw two fastballs. The third pitch was a curveball that the batter hit for a double.

Everyone at the game knew the pitcher hadn't done well. After all, he just gave up a double.

But Red Murff was thunderstruck. He didn't care about the curveball or the double. He knew he had seen one of the fastest hardballs ever thrown.

After the game, Red went up to the pitcher. "I just wanted to introduce myself," said Red. "I'm Red Murff. I scout for the New York Mets."

The young man shook his hand. "Nice to meet you," he said. "My name's Nolan Ryan."

That night Red watched a major league game in Houston. The two pitchers, Turk Farrell of Houston and Jim Maloney of the Cincinnati Reds, both had 95 mph fastballs. Red knew the tenth-grader he had seen earlier in the day threw harder than either of them.

Red filled out a scouting report for the Mets that night. He could hardly contain his excitement as he wrote. Nolan's fastball was "in the hundred-mile-per-hour range."

At the end of the high school season, Red went back to Alvin. He had a talk with Jim Watson, Nolan's baseball coach, and the high school athletic director.

He told them, "Ya'll have one of the ten best arms in the world in your school." Red stressed that they weren't to try to put Nolan in any kind of weight program or mess with his pitching arm. "Just let him throw the baseball."

Red told Coach Watson to have confidence in Nolan and to let him throw his fastball. He predicted Nolan would take Alvin to the state championship in Austin. From that day on, anytime Nolan pitched either Red or his assistant was there to watch.

Nolan wasn't sure what to think of Red's prediction. But he knew high school was a good time for him. He still thought he was a better basketball player than baseball player.

During the summer between his junior and senior year, Nolan, Ruth, and Mr. Ryan went to Colt Stadium in Houston to watch the new Houston major league team. That was the year before the Astrodome opened and the Colt .45s became the Astros.

The special attraction that day was Sandy Koufax pitching for the visiting Los Angeles Dodgers. Koufax was the best pitcher in baseball that year. Nolan was absolutely awestruck as he watched Koufax pitch with power and polish. He struck out eight batters and won the game. That experience added Koufax to Nolan's heroes. Before then his two biggest major league idols weren't pitchers. They were two outfielders—Hank Aaron and Roberto Clemente. What Nolan admired

15

about both of them was their hustle. They were both talented, but they also went all out on every play.

When Nolan's senior year rolled around, he couldn't wait for basketball season to start. As a junior he had led the team to a fantastic 27–4 record, including 18 straight wins. The season had been ruined by Clear Creek, a basketball powerhouse, that happened to be in Alvin's district. Clear Creek had won the district and kept Alvin out of the state playoffs. Nolan was determined that this year, his senior season, would be different.

But Nolan was wrong. The basketball season was almost identical to the one before. The Alvin Yellowjackets terrorized their opponents. They again posted a 27–4 record. Nolan was one of their stars. Clear Creek, however, wasn't about to give up their title. Once again they won the district and kept Alvin out of the playoffs.

What could be more frustrating? Had there ever been a team that went 54–8 over two seasons that didn't make the state playoffs? Nolan was frustrated, but he still had one final high school baseball season. Even though Alvin had never been a baseball powerhouse, perhaps in his senior year Nolan could lead them to the state playoffs. That's what Red Murff had predicted. Nolan was ready.

Nolan would be Alvin's workhorse. He shared the pitching duties with a junior, Pat Wagner. But anytime he had enough rest between games, Nolan would pitch. When he wasn't pitching, he played right field. He also batted clean-up.

16

By now, Nolan's reputation for his fastball and his wildness were legendary with the opposing teams. Batters were afraid of him. When Nolan pitched, Alvin usually won.

Now it was time for Nolan to be discovered by the major leagues. Red Murff was still watching Nolan pitch every game, but Red was just one of many scouts that the Mets had. He wanted his boss, Bing Devine, to see Nolan pitch. Red could hardly wait for Devine to see the pitching talent he had observed so closely for the past three years.

Disaster was about to strike. Alvin began district play. Even with Nolan, Alvin was expected to finish behind powerful Deer Park in the district. Alvin had two straight 1–0 losses.

Coach Watson was furious at his players. He ordered a punishment practice where all the players ran until they threw up. Then he made them take turns batting against Nolan, who was directed to pitch as hard as he could. By the end of the practice, all of the players were beyond exhaustion and Nolan's pitching arm was completely spent.

That's when Red called Coach Watson with the big news. Bing Devine was flying to Houston to watch Nolan pitch against Channelview High the next day. Coach Watson explained that Nolan was in no shape to pitch the next day, but Red insisted. "This is it," said Red. "This is his one shot to make the major leagues!"

The next day Alvin went to Channelview to play at a very plain field behind the high school. Bing Devine

17

and Red Murff were some of the few spectators in the small bleachers. Devine was ready to watch the fantastic high school pitcher that Red Murff had bragged on for the past three years.

Nolan took the mound. Even though he was tired, he was ready. This was his chance.

Nolan was awful. When he wasn't wild, he threw pitches that got hit. By the time Coach Watson replaced Nolan in the third inning, Alvin trailed 7–0.

Devine told Murff that he trusted him as a scout but that Nolan had obviously had a very bad day. He explained that he couldn't recommend Nolan as a draft choice for the Mets but that Murff would be free to try to make a case for Nolan to top management. Nolan had just blown his best shot at the majors.

That terrible game could have destroyed Nolan's confidence. It could have led to a collapse by the team. But it did just the opposite. The Alvin Yellowjackets and Nolan Ryan went on a roll. They won all the rest of their games, finishing the season with a 24–8 record, 8–2 in district. Nolan ended up the regular season 14–3 as a pitcher and hitting the ball as well. Deer Park, however, collapsed as the season ended. Alvin won district! They were in the state playoffs.

The playoff system was simple. Alvin would face another district winner in a best-of-three game series. The winner of that series would play best-of-three games with another team for the regional champi-

18

onship. That winner would advance to Austin for a single elimination tournament with three other teams to determine the state champion.

Alvin's first opponent was the El Campo Ricebirds. Nolan took the mound and pitched well but clearly didn't have his best stuff. Alvin led 1–0 in the second inning. With a mini-rally going, Alvin had runners on first and second. It was Nolan's turn to bat. This might not be his best pitching day of the year, but could he get the job done with his bat?

Nolan waited for his pitch. *Bang!* Nolan got a pitch right where he wanted it and smacked it. It cleared the fence for a three-run homer. Alvin led 4–0! Nolan's pitches got wild in the fifth and Pat Wagner finished the game, but the final score was Alvin 5, El Campo 1. Nolan was the winning pitcher, and his three-run homer had broken the game open.

Nolan pitched the next game, and Alvin won 3–1. They had beaten El Campo and were on to the regionals. There they would face Brenham. The schedule called for them to travel to Brenham for a doubleheader and then return to Alvin to play a third game, if needed.

While the playoffs were beginning, school ended. Nolan graduated and was named Outstanding Athlete at Alvin High. Red Murff called and told Nolan he'd been drafted by the Mets after all, not in the first or even second round, but the thirteenth. He was the 295th pick. Professional baseball thought there were 294 players better than Nolan. In fact, Red Murff was the only scout who believed in Nolan. All the others suggested he try playing college baseball first.

Nolan put his disappointment with the major league draft behind him. School was over and he could concentrate on baseball—high school baseball. He had played well against El Campo, but his pitching had been only average. He was ready to prove something against Brenham.

Nolan took the mound against Brenham. Brenham had a better team than El Campo, and Nolan knew he needed to pitch well. No one was disappointed. Nolan was simply overwhelming. When the game ended, Nolan had struck out 16 and Alvin had won, 2–1.

Pat Wagner pitched well in the second game, but Brenham won. That tied the series at 1–1. The deciding game would be played two days later in Alvin. Nolan would have some rest for his arm and be ready to pitch. Alvin's hope was going to ride on Nolan's arm.

Nolan had totally dominated the Brenham hitters in the first game. He was even better in the second. For seven innings, Brenham hitters tried to figure out how to hit Nolan's fastball. They never did. Nolan pitched a no-hitter. Brenham did scratch out one unearned run, but Alvin scored three. Nolan had contributed a double and scored one of the runs. Alvin was headed to Austin for the championship! At least one of Red Murff's predictions had come true.

The state tournament was held at Disch Field, the

home of Austin's minor league team, the Braves. The class AAA favorite was the South San Antonio Bobcats. The Bobcats, who had won the state championship five times, were coached by Cliff Gustafson. Gustafson would soon leave to coach the University of Texas and later become the winningest coach in college baseball history.

The Bobcats were 37–2 coming into the tournament. Fortunately, for Alvin, their first game was to be against Snyder. Waxahachie had the dubious honor of having to play South San Antonio. The winners of the first two games would play the following day for the state title.

When Nolan went to the mound against Snyder, he knew this was nothing like regular high school ball. This was in a real baseball stadium. Instead of a handful of spectators, there were 1,200 fans who wanted to see a good ballgame.

Nolan came out ready to do his best. For five innings, he pitched a no-hitter. Snyder's pitching was also very good. The sixth inning began as a scoreless tie. Alvin's first baseman, Donald Green, reached first on an infield ground ball. Third baseman Billy Childress then made a sacrifice bunt but was safe at first on an error.

With two runners on, Nolan came to the plate. Nolan knew that this might be Alvin's best chance to score. He knew that the game was riding not only on his arm but on his bat. Nolan wanted a fastball. It came. *Whap!* He drilled it down the left field line for a double. Green scored. One run. Childress scored. Two runs. Alvin had the lead.

In the bottom of the sixth, Nolan kept up his no-hitter for the first two outs. Then Snyder broke through with back-to-back singles. Nolan took a deep breath. Two outs, two on. He had a two-run lead. But one bad pitch and the game could be tied or worse.

No problem. Nolan struck the next batter out.

Alvin added a run in the top of the seventh. Nolan finished Snyder off in their last at bat. Alvin won 3-0. They were in the state championship game! Luck was also on their side: South San Antonio had lost to Waxahachie. The championship was in Alvin's reach.

Coach Watson had a tough decision to make. Should he pitch Nolan the next day against Waxahachie or let Pat Wagner have the start? Pat had had a good year, but Nolan had been the only pitcher to win in the playoffs. Watson remembered Nolan's disastrous start against Channelview when he had pitched without rest. He thought about all the possibilities and then decided. If Alvin was to win, it would be with Nolan Ryan on the mound.

Nolan was a great high school pitcher, but superman he was not. He lasted only four batters against Waxahachie before Coach Watson took him out. Waxahachie got three runs that inning. Although Alvin refused to give up, the game was over before it started. The final score was Waxahachie 6, Alvin 3.

That final loss hardly seemed to matter. Alvin finished second in the state. Nolan Ryan had been a dominating player. He won five games in the state tournament, pitched a no-hitter, and batted .700. He was named to the All-State team and finished the season with a 20–3 record.

It was a great way to finish high school. High school had been fun. It had been everything Nolan had dreamed about. But now he had to decide about his future—a future beyond the safe confines of Alvin, Texas.

The choices were clear. Either go to college and play sports—maybe basketball and baseball—or sign with the Mets. College sounded pretty good to Nolan. He could stay near home and play sports. Besides, Nolan wasn't very happy about professional baseball drafting him number 295.

Red Murff wasn't going to give up. He talked the Mets into offering Nolan $20,000 to sign. That kind of money was offered to players drafted much earlier.

Mr. Ryan thought Nolan should sign with the Mets. In fact, everyone but Nolan was convinced.

Finally, on June 28, Red brought the contract to the Ryans' house. Mr. and Mrs. Ryan, Nolan, Red, and a newspaper reporter from Texas City, Steve Vernon, sat at the kitchen table. The reporter had been allowed in by Mrs. Ryan on the condition that he not say a word.

The five of them sat at the table. Red made his offer. Everyone sat silently and just looked at Nolan.

No one knew what to do next. So they sat there in silence. Waiting.

Steve Vernon finally broke. "What's the matter with you, boy?" he cried as he jumped out of his chair. "You crazy? Sign!"

It was just the nudge Nolan needed. He signed.

Nolan didn't have much time to say goodbye. Red got him a plane ticket for Bristol, Tennessee, and told him to get from there to Marion, Tennessee, home of a brand new single-A minor league team for the Mets.

Nolan's mother and Ruth took him to the airport in Houston. This was to be Nolan's first plane ride, and the first time he had really been away from home. They said their goodbyes, and Nolan walked across the runway and took the stairs up to the plane.

As the plane took off, Nolan looked down and saw Houston and then looked toward Alvin. Everything he had known was back there on the ground. He was off on a trip to an unknown future. But he knew one thing for sure—his future was going to be baseball.

BUS RIDE THROUGH
THE MINORS

1965–1967

3

BRISTOL, TENNESSEE. NOLAN had changed planes in Atlanta and had flown to this small city in the Appalachian Mountains in the far eastern part of Tennessee.

Nolan wanted to be confident. Nolan wanted to be a success. Nolan wanted to leave his mark in the baseball world. But the reality was that Nolan was just an 18-year-old kid away from home for the first time. He certainly wasn't going to get any confidence boost on that first day.

"Marion? Son, there is no Marion in the whole state of Tennessee."

It didn't matter who he asked. The answer was the same. No one at the airport could help. There simply was no Marion in the state.

There is one thing an 18-year-old boy doesn't want

to do on his first day in the adult world—call home for help. But that was Nolan's only choice. He called his mother.

A few phone calls later and the confusion was settled. The Marion team was brand new, and Red Murff had just assumed that since the airport was in Tennessee so was the team. Wrong. Marion was in Virginia, a two-hour car ride through the mountains from the Bristol airport.

The confusion was settled. Nolan found the right state and the right town. He arrived in Marion, Virginia, a small town about the size of Alvin, ready to begin his professional baseball career.

Nolan found a room to rent from a widow who rented out some of the bedrooms of her large house. Nolan quickly settled in, but he was anxious to report to the baseball team.

"Uniform? Sure kid, we'll get you one as soon as it becomes available."

From Little League through high school, Nolan had always been given a uniform when he joined a team. Not so in professional baseball. You might have been a big star at home, but at a rookie league team like Marion the new guys waited for a uniform to become available.

Nolan only waited a few days. He got a uniform. But there was one problem. It came from a short player. Nolan, standing 6 foot 2 inches, certainly wasn't short. Oh, well. Nolan pulled his socks all the way up. They barely reached the bottom of his pants. At least he had a uniform.

Nolan quickly learned one rookie-league lesson. Every kid on the Marion team was a star, a hometown hero. But at Marion, they all had to wait for a uniform. Every time a new "star" arrived, one of the other "stars" had to be cut from the team. That's how a uniform became available.

Over that summer, Nolan watched as 70 players came to Marion full of dreams. Most of them were sent home, cut from the team, so that a uniform would be available for the next kid.

It may be every Little Leaguer's dream to play professional baseball. But the rookie league was not a place where dreams came true. It was a place where dreams were crushed.

Nolan was determined not to have his dream end in Marion. He found rookie league baseball very difficult. There were long bus rides, bad fields, dim lights, and small dressing rooms in all the towns Marion played. But throughout the summer, Nolan threw his fastball. Some nights he was wild, some nights he gave up too many walks, but he was always fast.

The real highlight of Nolan's summer wasn't on the baseball field. It was a visit from his girlfriend, Ruth. She had persuaded her father to drive her to Virginia for a visit. Nolan missed home, but mostly he missed Ruth.

Nolan wasn't the kind of kid who forgot his parents. He had $20,000 in bonus money. He could have blown it on things for himself. Instead, he kept thinking how hard his father would have to work for that kind of money. He finally decided to pay off the mortgage on his parents' home with his signing money. It was a way to say thanks for all his parents had done for him.

While the mortgage took most of his bonus, Nolan had a few thousand left. He decided on one luxury—a new car. He went to the Chevy dealer and bought a brand new 1965 Impala. Maroon with red interior.

When Ruth visited him that summer, she found the same old Nolan. But he was growing more confident. And he loved driving her around in his brand new Impala.

Nolan lasted the whole season at Marion. He won 3 games and lost 6. He had walked 56 batters and hit 8 more. But his win-loss record and walks weren't what mattered. What did matter was his manager's evaluation of him.

Peter Pavelick, a veteran baseball manager, saw plenty of potential in Nolan. He was impressed that Nolan had 115 strikeouts in 78 innings. He wrote positive reports about Nolan. When the season was over at Marion, Nolan was one of 20 Mets players sent to Florida to play in the winter instructional league.

Nolan reported to St. Petersburg, Florida, for the winter league. His manager, Eddie Stanky, was strict and tough. But the atmosphere was totally different from Marion. Here the players were taught and encouraged, not cut.

For the first time, Nolan had a real pitching coach. He could see that he had a lot to learn before he could be a major league pitcher. But now he was being taught what he needed to know. He learned that pitching was more than just throwing hard; he had to outthink the hitters.

When the instructional league ended, Nolan went to Homestead, another Florida town, for minor league spring training. At Homestead, he met Tom Seaver. Seaver had just finished a fabulous career in college pitching for the University of Southern California. He was older and more experienced than Nolan, and everyone knew he was the Mets' star of the future.

After spring training, all of the Mets' minor leaguers would be assigned to teams in either the single-A, double-A, or triple-A leagues. Triple-A was for the best players; it was the last stop before the major leagues. Nolan was sent to Greenville, North Carolina, a single-A team. Seaver was sent to Jacksonville, a triple-A team.

Greenville may have been a promotion from Marion, but everything else was the same. Long bus rides, rough fields, bad lights, and cramped dressing rooms. One good thing was that Pete Pavelick had also moved from Marion to Greenville, so Nolan at least had the same manager.

Nolan had learned a lot in the instructional league, and it showed. He was simply overpowering to the hitters in the single-A Western Carolina League. When the season ended, he had struck out 272 batters and won 17 games while losing only two.

His best game of the season was when Ruth came to visit. This time she came with Nolan's parents and one of his sisters. It was a seven-inning game against Gastonia. Nolan struck out an incredible 19 batters—out of 21 possible outs.

It was the kind of season that got Nolan some attention. Newspapers started comparing Nolan to Sandy Koufax, the best pitcher of the day. Koufax was not only a strikeout ace but had pitched an amazing four no-hit games.

The Mets also noticed Nolan's great season. The double-A season lasted longer than the single-A season, so when single-A ended Nolan was promoted to double-A Williamsport.

Williamsport, every Little Leaguer's dream, not only hosted the Little League World Series but also had a double-A ball club. He may not have made it as a Little Leaguer, but Nolan was just as happy to be there.

Nolan was happy—but the double-A batters weren't. Nolan stayed there for 10 days and pitched in three games for a total of 19 innings. In those 19 innings, he struck out an incredible 35 batters—nearly two batters an inning. He gave up only two earned runs, giving him a fantastic earned run average of 0.95.

Fortunately, for the double-A batters, major league baseball has a special rule that allows teams to add a few minor leaguers to their team rosters for the last month of the season. This allows the stars of the future to get a taste of major league baseball. Most times they sit on the bench. Sometimes they get to pitch a couple of times or bat some in games that don't affect the team's chances to win a championship.

The Mets called Nolan up to play with the big league team for September. Nolan was going to see how his fastball worked against the very best hitters in baseball.

The Mets had been created as an expansion team in 1962. As a team, they were awful. In 1966 they finished 30 games behind first-place Los Angeles.

But the Mets were loved by their fans. They were the lovable losers who shared a city with the legendary Yankees. The Mets played in a beautiful new park, Shea Stadium, and regularly had 25,000 fans turn out for their games.

Nolan's month with the Mets showed him the way baseball could be played. Gone were the minors with long bus trips, bad lights, rough fields, and cold showers. Now he was in a world of airplanes, great playing fields, and fantastic dressing rooms.

On September 11, 1966, Nolan got his first chance to pitch. He was called on to pitch two innings of relief against the Atlanta Braves. Nolan got his first major league strikeout against the Atlanta pitcher Pat Jarvis and also struck out Eddie Mathews and Dennis Menke. Braves slugger Hank Aaron would later say that Nolan had one of the best fastballs he had ever seen.

But as hard as he threw, he soon found out that a fastball wasn't going to be enough against major league batters. Nolan threw a really hard fastball to Joe Torre, who took a big swing and knocked it out of the park. Nolan knew then that he would need a lot more than just a fastball to make it in the majors.

The Mets decided to see what would happen if Nolan started a game. His first big league start was set in Houston at the Astrodome on September 18. Nolan was going to pitch just 30 miles from his home in Alvin.

The Astrodome, called the eighth wonder of the world when it opened in 1965, was the first domed stadium. On September 18 it was filled with folks from Alvin. There were Nolan's parents, his sisters, Ruth, his high school coach Jim Watson, and a good part of the rest of the town.

It seemed everyone in the Astrodome that day was rooting for the Mets, or at least for Nolan. But the Astro hitters didn't pay any attention to that. Nolan lasted only one inning, and the Astros scored three runs on him.

It wasn't what Nolan or his fans had hoped for. But there was one bit of good news. If the Astro players didn't get a hit or walk off Nolan, he struck them out. In fact, all three outs in the first inning came on strikeouts. Everyone could see Nolan had the talent to be a success in the majors. He just needed more time to develop.

Nolan went back to Alvin after the season and took

classes at Alvin Community College. With the Vietnam War nearing its peak years, all young men had to fulfill a military obligation. Nolan entered the Army Reserves in January. He missed spring training and the beginning of the season as he learned to be a soldier at Fort Jackson, South Carolina, and Fort Leonard Wood, Missouri.

After completing nearly six months of training, Nolan's full-time army service was over. He still had to report for occasional weekend and summer duty, but he was free to return to baseball.

The Mets immediately assigned Nolan to their Winter Haven team to get in shape. Nolan pitched four innings in Winter Haven, striking out five and allowing only one run.

Then Nolan went to triple-A Jacksonville. The Mets planned on giving Nolan time to learn to pitch in triple-A ball. Bill Virdon, the Jacksonville manager who had also managed Nolan for his brief time at Williamsport, wanted to bring Nolan along slowly.

Virdon limited Nolan to seven innings in three games. Nolan was on fire. He struck out 18 batters in those seven innings and didn't allow a single earned run. Nolan was on track for a great season.

Nolan was scheduled to start a home game in Jacksonville. The fans wanted to see Nolan and his amazing fastball. The game was sold out.

But as Nolan was warming up, disaster struck. Something in his pitching arm popped. Pain shot through his arm whenever he tried to pitch. The sold-out crowd had their money refunded and most of them went home.

Nolan spent the rest of the season in Jacksonville working to rehabilitate his arm. But he had thrown his last pitch for 1967. The season that began with great promise was over before it started.

Still, there would be great happiness for Nolan in 1967. Ruth had graduated from high school. She and Nolan decided to get married.

The Mets didn't want to give Nolan any time off during the season—even if he was injured and even if he was going to get married. They finally agreed he could get married on a Monday if he returned on Tuesday.

The wedding was set for Monday, June 26, 1967. It was a big church wedding at the Alvin Methodist Church. The wedding took place without any problems, except that Nolan's father had become ill the morning of the ceremony and had to be hospitalized. Nolan and Ruth finished with all their family and friends, the photographer, the cake and the punch, and then headed straight for the hospital.

Mr. Ryan was groggy from all the medicine he had been given. He couldn't talk, but he did nod and blink and squeeze Nolan's hand. The doctors assured Nolan that his father would be all right and home in a few days.

But Nolan knew that while his dad might survive for the moment, he was dying of cancer. It was the price he paid for a lifetime of cigarette smoking. He had a lot of medical problems caused by his smoking.

Nolan had watched his dad smoke all the years he was growing up. He knew the cigarettes would kill him. It convinced Nolan that he never wanted to smoke.

As they left the hospital, the newlyweds hopped into Nolan's maroon Impala. It had been decorated with white shoe polish letters and tin cans tied to its bumper. The only food they had eaten all day had been wedding cake and punch. They were starved. So, even though it was their wedding night, Nolan and Ruth did what any true Texas teenagers would do in the same situation. They found a fast-food restaurant. They went into the drive-thru and loaded up with hamburgers, fries, and Cokes. So much for a fancy meal on their wedding night!

Nolan didn't pitch the rest of the 1967 season, and his arm slowly got better. The Mets sent him to the instructional league to play winter ball. His velocity and strength soon returned.

Nolan went to spring training full of hope for the 1968 season. So did the Mets. While they had never been a very good ball club, they had a lot of promising players and great fan support. In 1967, Tom Seaver had a 16–13 record, struck out 170 batters, and won the Rookie of the Year Award. The Mets were anxious to bring Nolan and another young pitching prospect, Jerry Koosman, up to the majors to be that year's Tom Seaver.

Most everyone who knew baseball knew Nolan could use another year in triple-A ball. This was especially true because he was going to miss a lot of starts due to his military obligations. But newspapers and fans were comparing Nolan not just to Tom Seaver but to Sandy Koufax and every other great pitcher. They were ready to see his fastball against the greatest hitters in the game.

The Mets made their decision. Nolan would be in a Mets uniform on opening day. He would never pitch in the minors again.

THE AMAZING METS

1968–1971

Aᴌʟ ᴏꜰ ᴛʜᴇ ᴍᴀᴊᴏʀ leagues are big time. But New York City is like no other city. It is the largest city in the United States and has the newspapers, TV, and radio shows to prove it. New Yorkers are fanatics about their sports.

The Mets were a special case for New Yorkers. Their other teams, the Yankees, the basketball Knicks, and the football Giants were known as winners. The Mets became known as lovable losers—but losers all the same. Since they began in 1962, they had never finished better than next to last. Still, they drew more fans than the Yankees.

Mets fans had hopes of the Mets becoming winners. When Tom Seaver won the Rookie of the Year Award in 1967, expectations for the future rose.

The fans were hoping Nolan could repeat Seaver's performance in 1968. They expected it from him. So did the news media. Nolan Ryan was to produce big things and he was to do it right away. The pressure was on.

Manager Gil Hodges decided Nolan would be one of his five starting pitchers. Nolan would pitch every fifth game.

Luckily, Nolan's first start would be on the road, away from the pressure in New York City. Unluckily, it was going to be in the Astrodome—the same place he had his disastrous outing in 1966.

Nolan was ready. The Easter Sunday crowd of 15,000 fans in the Astrodome were ready too. The Astros were hot. They had won their first four games of the season. The fans wanted this to be number five. Larry Dierker, the Astros' young pitching star, had already won his first start of the season and was pitching again today.

Nolan stood off the pitcher's mound as he listened to "The Star-Spangled Banner." He knew his father, three sisters, and a lot of friends from Alvin were in the stands. He knew he had to do better than he did in 1966.

When the music stopped, Nolan took the mound. He put everything out of his mind. Nolan focused on pitching and pitching only.

Ron Davis, the Astro centerfielder, was the first batter. Nolan looked at his catcher, Jerry Grote. Grote flashed him the sign for a fastball. Nolan went through

38

his wind-up and delivered his pitch. *Thwap!* The sound of the fastball hitting Grote's glove could be heard in the stands. "Strike one!" shouted the home plate umpire. That was followed by "Strike two!" and "Strike three!" Davis sat down as Nolan's first strikeout victim of the day. He wouldn't be the last.

Next up was second baseman Joe Morgan. Same result. Morgan struck out and sat down.

Next came rightfielder Norm Miller. Nolan struck him out too.

Nolan ran off the field to the Mets' dugout. He had been untouchable. He not only struck out the side, but the Astro hitters hadn't even managed a foul ball.

It wasn't until the second batter in the second inning that an Astro finally hit a foul ball. The Astrodome crowd broke out in wild applause when Rusty Staub managed to at least touch a Nolan Ryan fastball.

Nolan kept it up all afternoon. He struck out seven of the first ten batters. After five innings, Nolan had a no-hitter going.

Larry Dierker was pitching well too. But the Mets managed to score one run in both the second and fourth innings.

Nolan took the mound to begin the sixth inning. A blister was developing on the middle finger of his right hand, but he was still throwing well.

Pinch hitter Lee Thomas came to the plate. He was determined to get his bat on the ball and break up the no-hitter. Thomas got the pitch he wanted and knocked a bloop single to left field. That ended the no-hitter. One out later, Joe Morgan singled up the middle. Hal King hit a weak ground ball in front of the plate. He was thrown out but moved Thomas and Morgan up to second and third base.

Next up was Rusty Staub. Rusty was always a good hitter. With two runners in scoring position, all Staub needed was a single and the game would be tied.

The pressure was really on now. One bad pitch and Nolan's great first five innings would be for nothing. Nolan knew what he had to do.

He looked at Grote for the sign. Grote wanted a fastball, outside, away from Staub's power. Nolan knew it was time to reach deep down inside. He wound up and delivered his hardest pitch of the day. *Thwap!* Fastball on the outside corner. Right where Grote wanted it. "Strike one!"

Nolan checked the sign again. Grote wanted the same pitch. Nolan delivered again. *Thwap!* Right where Grote wanted it. "Strike two!"

Nolan checked Grote's sign again. Fastball, outside corner. Nolan couldn't believe it. His curveball and change-up had been working well that day. But Grote knew Staub would be thinking change or curve and he wanted to fool him with a third straight fastball.

Nolan checked the runners on second and third base. He knew he couldn't make a mistake. He delivered the pitch. *Thwap!* "Strike three!" Nolan had proved he could pitch out of a jam. Now he knew he belonged in the majors.

With two outs in the seventh inning, the blister on Nolan's finger was really bothering him. Manager Gil Hodges came to the mound and decided Nolan had pitched enough. Reliever Danny Frisella finished the game. When it was over, the Mets won 4–0. Nolan struck out eight and gave up only three hits. He had his first major league victory!

Five days later, Nolan took the mound in Shea Stadium for his first start in front of the New York fans. Just as in Houston, Nolan's fastball was on fire. He struck out the first three Dodgers using only nine pitches. Unfortunately, his Met teammates were not going to have a good day at the plate. Nolan pitched six shutout innings but gave up one run in the seventh and two in the eighth when he was lifted for a relief pitcher. He struck out 11 Dodgers but lost the game, with the final score Dodgers 3, Mets 2.

Nolan's next start was against the Reds in Cincinnati. Nolan pitched superbly, but his teammates committed four errors giving up four runs on just one base hit. Nolan ended up with seven strikeouts but was the losing pitcher.

Nolan's pitching was too good to keep losing games. He won his next two starts. He struck out ten Phillies in six innings in a 3–0 win for the Mets. Then he went to St. Louis and pitched his first complete game in the major leagues. It was a jewel as he struck out eight Cardinals and allowed only three hits in a 4–1 win.

41

Next up were the Reds, this time in New York City. Nolan sizzled. When he was done, he owned the Mets' club record for most strikeouts in a single game with 14. He pitched the whole nine innings and won the game 3–2.

The pressure had really been on Nolan. But he delivered. One month into the season Nolan was 4–2 and led the National League in strikeouts with 58.

But the fairytale season would soon end. Nolan still had military duty on weekends. Nolan missed a lot of his chances to pitch. This made it harder for him to keep in practice. Plus, Nolan's blister kept bothering him. The trainers tried everything—even had Nolan soak his hand in pickle brine—but the blister kept coming back.

To make matters worse, Nolan was worried about his father's health. In July his father had to have surgery. The doctors removed his left lung.

Nolan missed the entire month of August. First, his blister put him on the disabled list. Then he had two weeks of military duty.

When Nolan came back to the Mets, he was no longer a starter. Manager Gil Hodges used him only as a relief pitcher and only put him into hopeless situations. Nolan ended up losing his last five decisions. The last two months of the season, Nolan had only three strikeouts, the same number he got in the first inning of his first game of the season.

Nolan ended his first full major league season with a disappointing 6–9 record. The Mets finished in ninth place, 24 games behind the champion St. Louis Cardinals. The season that began with so much promise had completely fallen apart. He was happy to get back to Alvin for the off-season. He could only hope that 1969 would be better.

Unfortunately, 1969 began the same way 1968 ended. Nolan was bothered by his finger blister, and his military duty kept interrupting his pitching. He needed to learn a lot but wasn't learning anything. He was being used mainly as a relief pitcher. Nolan was frustrated.

By the time Nolan left for three weeks of summer military duty in August, he had a decent 5–1 record but still felt discouraged. He had pitched few innings, and he hated being a relief pitcher. The Mets, while they weren't in their usual last place, were nine and a half games behind the Cubs, who had been in first place since the beginning of the season.

But while Nolan was on military duty, one of the most incredible stories in sports history began. The Mets, losers who had never finished better than next to last place, were transformed into the Amazing Mets— a team that was unstoppable.

The Mets won 20 of their next 26 ballgames. They were a half-game behind the Cubs. On September 10 the Cubs were playing the Phillies, and the Mets had a doubleheader against the Expos. The Cubs lost their game 6–2. The Mets won their first game 3–2 in 12

43

innings. That made the second game critical. If the Mets lost they would be tied for first place with the Cubs. If the Mets won, they would be in sole possession of first place—a place the Mets had never been.

Manager Gil Hodges looked at his pitching staff. He decided to give Nolan a rare chance to be a starting pitcher.

Nolan wasn't going to waste his chance. He pitched the whole nine-inning game. He allowed just three hits while striking out 11. Nolan and the Mets won, 7–1. The Mets—the Amazing Mets—were in first place!

Through the rest of September 1969, the Mets continued their winning ways. They ended up in first place, eight games ahead of second-place Chicago. Nolan finished with a good 6–3 record, but he pitched only 89 innings the entire season.

The season wasn't over quite yet. The playoffs were just beginning.

In 1969 the National League had added the Montreal Expos and San Diego Padres to the league just as they added the Mets and Astros in 1962. But with 12 teams in the league they divided into a couple of six-team divisions. The Mets won the East division; the Atlanta Braves won the West division. The two teams would play a best-of-five series to determine which team would be the National League Champion and play in the World Series.

The first two games against the Braves were played in Atlanta. Tom Seaver and Jerry Koosman were the

Mets' starting pitchers. In both games the Mets used relief pitchers, but Hodges chose not to use Nolan. The Mets won both games.

The series moved to New York. Rookie Gary Gentry was starting for the Mets.

Shea Stadium was packed with a standing-room-only crowd. After eight years of rooting for a losing team, the fans were hungry for a victory. The Braves had other ideas. Future Hall of Famer Hank Aaron hit a two-run homer in the first.

Gentry held the Braves in check in the second. He began the third inning trailing 2–0. Centerfielder Tony Gonzalez led off with a single. Aaron followed with a double that sent Gonzalez to third. Clean-up batter Rico Carty took a 1–1 pitch and slammed a hard liner foul down the left field line.

Manager Hodges had seen enough. He went to the pitcher's mound and signaled to the bullpen. He wanted Nolan.

Nolan took the mound and began throwing his warm-up pitches. This was the break he had waited for all season. But it was a very difficult situation. Runners on second and third, no outs, the Braves' hottest hitter at the plate, and his team already down by two runs. To top it off, there were 50,000 screaming fans and a nationwide TV audience. This was real pressure.

Nolan cleared it all from his mind. This was baseball, and he was standing on a pitcher's mound.

Nolan looked at his catcher Jerry Grote. He got the sign for a fastball. The count was 1–2. Carty stood in the batter's box. Nolan checked the runners, and began his delivery. *Thwap!* Nolan delivered a perfect fastball to the lower outside corner of the strike zone. "Strike three!" screamed the umpire. The fans went wild.

But there was still only one out. Hodges sent in the signal to intentionally walk the next batter, Orlando Cepeda. That loaded the bases. Now Nolan had to be very careful because a walk would mean a run. No problem. He struck out Clete Boyer and got Bob Didier to pop out. As Nolan ran off the mound the fans rose— all 50,000 of them—to give him a standing ovation.

The Mets scored one run in the bottom of the third. They scored two more in the fourth to take a 3–2 lead. In the fifth, Nolan made a bad pitch to Orlando Cepeda. Cepeda walloped a two-run homer to put the Braves up 4–3. But the Mets responded with three runs in the bottom of the fifth and added another one in the sixth.

Nolan didn't make any more mistakes. When the game was over, he had pitched seven innings, allowed three hits, and struck out seven while allowing only the two runs on Cepeda's homer. Final score was Mets 7, Braves 3. The Mets were the National League Champions. Next stop—the World Series!

The Baltimore Orioles were a big favorite to win that World Series. They had three nearly unbeatable pitching aces—Jim Palmer, Dave McNally, and Mike Cuellar—along with a heavy hitting lineup that included Frank Robinson, Brooks Robinson, and Boog Powell. The Orioles were so confident that they bragged about how they were going to end the Mets' miracle season.

The series opened in Baltimore. The first Oriole batter took Tom Seaver's first pitch and sent it over the fence for a home run. It looked like Baltimore would cream the Mets. But the Amazing Mets still had life in them. When they left Baltimore, the series was tied at one game each.

Back in New York, game three was played in front of a huge, standing-room-only crowd. Mets' management sold every place to stand and crammed more than 56,000 fans into Shea Stadium.

Gary Gentry started for the Mets. He wasn't pitching very well, but the Orioles couldn't score a run and the Mets were hitting well. By the seventh inning, the Mets led 4–0.

Nolan watched the game from the bullpen. He was happy for the team, but he wanted to be a pitcher not a spectator. This was Seaver, Koosman, and Gentry's World Series. If a late inning reliever was needed it would be Tug McGraw or Ron Taylor. Nolan was the forgotten man on the pitching staff.

But with two outs in the seventh, Gentry lost control. He walked one batter, then another, and finally a third. The bases were loaded and Gentry couldn't find the strike zone.

Hodges came out to the mound and took the ball from Gentry. He signaled to the bullpen for the right-hander. Nolan was going to get a chance.

47

Nolan could scarcely believe it. Here was a crucial situation in the World Series, and Hodges was turning to him.

Nolan knew what to do. There were 56,000 fans screaming "Let's go, Mets! Let's go, Mets!" in nonstop unison. The pressure was unbelievable. But Nolan cleared his mind and focused on pitching.

The batter was centerfielder Paul Blair. He was a good, disciplined hitter who seldom struck out.

Nolan got the sign from Grote, checked the runner at third, and delivered a low fastball. *Thwap!* It hit Grote's glove. "Strike one!" On the next pitch, Ryan came with another fastball. *Thwap!* "Strike two!"

Ryan was ahead in the count 0–2. The smart thing for a pitcher to do with that count is to throw a pitch just outside of the strike zone and hope the batter swings. Or the pitcher might throw a hard inside pitch to set up an outside strike for the next pitch. But Nolan was young and impatient. The crowd was going crazy. He decided to come right at Blair with a third straight fastball.

Nolan delivered the pitch. Blair was waiting. *Crack!* Blair hit a hard line drive to the gap in right center—a sure double that would bring in three runners.

Ah, but this was the Amazing Mets. Rightfielder Tommie Agee took off after the ball. At the last second, he dove. He caught the ball inches off the ground as he skidded on one knee.

The fans went wild! But no one felt like cheering more than Nolan. He had made a bad mistake—a mistake a thinking pitcher should never make. Agee had saved him from disaster.

Nolan got through the eighth inning without giving up any runs. The Mets' Ed Kranepool hit a solo homer in the bottom of the eighth. Nolan and the Mets held a 5–0 lead going into the ninth.

Nolan retired the first two batters with flyballs. One out to go. But Nolan walked Mark Belanger, Clay Dalrymple had an infield single, and then Nolan walked Don Buford. The bases were loaded.

Gil Hodges walked slowly to the mound. Hodges never had much patience when Nolan was walking batters. "You got anything left?" he asked Nolan. Nolan assured him he did. "Go get 'em," was all he said as he let Nolan stay in.

The next batter was Paul Blair. Nolan threw two straight fastballs past him for strikes. He now had Blair in the same position he had been in two innings earlier. Nolan was not going to make the same mistake twice. There was not going to be another fastball.

Grote flashed Nolan the sign for a curveball. Nolan thought that was fine, but he wanted it to be in the strike zone. Nolan reared back exactly as though he was delivering a fastball. He threw his best curveball of the day. Blair stood there frozen and surprised. "Strike three!" yelled the ump.

The Mets won the game. They now led the series 2–1. Nolan and Tommie Agee were the heroes of the game.

The Mets went on to win games 4 and 5. The Amazing Mets were now World Champions!

The story of the 1969 Mets is one of the greatest stories in sports history. The lovable losers—whose best previous finish had been ninth place—suddenly became the World Champs.

Americans love underdogs. There couldn't be a better underdog story than this one. Fans nationwide embraced the Amazing Mets, and New York fans went absolutely wild.

The team appeared on Ed Sullivan's popular national TV show. New York City gave the Mets a tickertape parade.

Imagine Nolan Ryan, a 22-year-old from a small Texas town, riding on the back of a new convertible through the middle of a skyscraper canyon in downtown Manhattan. Tens of thousands of fans screamed. The sky was filled with tickertape and paper from the offices high above.

Such attention could go to a player's head. But not Nolan's. He had never forgotten Alvin or his roots. He was the kind of kid who flew his parents to New York to see the World Series. Once the hoopla was over, he headed straight back for Alvin.

Other players spent the whole off-season in New York making as much money from personal appearances as they could. Nolan just wanted to get back to Texas for the start of hunting season.

There was a $20,000 World Series bonus for each Mets player. Nolan and Ruth bought their first house and eight acres of land just outside of Alvin.

Nolan began the 1970 season by pitching a near no-hitter against the Phillies. He ended up giving up just one hit and striking out 15—a team record. But the 1970 season turned out to be disappointing for both the Mets and Nolan.

The Mets didn't even win their division. Nolan finished with a disappointing 7–11 record. Worse still, he had walked 97 batters in 132 innings. That was way too many walks for a major league pitcher.

But the worst part of 1970 was personal. Nolan's father died that summer.

Nolan's dad had been the anchor in his life. He hadn't given Nolan much in the way of material things, but he had given him his values. Those values allowed Nolan to handle the pressure and the temptations of professional baseball. Nolan relied on his dad for advice and talked over important decisions with him.

Nolan took his father's death very hard. He became so discouraged, he thought about quitting baseball. Ruth convinced him to give it some more time. She knew Nolan would eventually be the success he wanted to be.

The first half of the 1971 season looked promising for Nolan. The trainers had finally solved his finger blister problem and he was back as a regular starting pitcher. In May he struck out 16 in a game against San Diego. He had an 8–4 record by the end of June.

But the second half of the season was a disaster. Nolan's pitching fell apart. He went into a terrible slump, finishing the season with just two more wins and 10 losses. Worse still, he walked 116 batters.

Nolan had pitched four full years with the Mets. His record was 29 wins, 38 losses. He was getting wilder and his walk total was awful. Nolan wasn't enjoying baseball. He knew something had to change.

He went to the general manager and asked for a trade. Maybe a fresh start somewhere else? Maybe a new pitching coach? Maybe something else? Nolan knew he could be a great pitcher, but it wasn't going to happen with the Mets.

Nolan and Ruth had one wonderful thing happen after the season. Their first son, Reid, was born in Houston on November 21. Two weeks later they got another piece of good news. Nolan and three other players had been traded to the California Angels for All-Star infielder Jim Fregosi.

The Ryans were heading for sunny southern California. Nolan was going to get his fresh start. Perhaps there he could be the successful pitcher he knew he could be.

A FRESH START

1972

NOLAN'S FRESH START IN sunny California began a lot like his troubled times with the Mets had ended.

To begin with, the news media was very critical of the Angels for trading an All-Star like Fregosi for an unproven pitcher like Ryan. Fregosi had been popular with the fans and the media. The nicest thing the media said about the trade was that it was "foolish."

Then, in spring training, Nolan's pitching was awful. He was having trouble controlling his pitches and became wilder and wilder. The harder he tried, the wilder he became.

To make matters worse, there was a players' strike. The players didn't get paid during the strike. Nolan and Ruth had a new baby to take care of and were broke. Nolan had to borrow money from a bank just to pay his bills.

Nolan was at the lowest point of his career. He began to think he really wasn't cut out to be in the majors. He hated to borrow money. Once again, Ruth had to talk him into not quitting. Fortunately, the strike ended quickly.

But it wasn't all tough times for Nolan as he began with the Angels. Management believed in Nolan. Both general manager Harry Dalton and team manager Del Rice were convinced Nolan could be a star.

Also, Nolan met Jimmie Reese. Jimmie, one of the California coaches, had been in baseball his whole life. As a player he had roomed with Babe Ruth. He was considerably older than Nolan, but they quickly developed a special friendship. Jimmie became Nolan's confidant as well as a coach.

Nolan also had a great pitching coach in Tom Morgan. Morgan knew pitching and he knew how to make a good pitcher better. Added to Morgan's coaching was Jeff Torborg's catching. Torborg may have been a player, but he was as good as having another coach for a pitcher. Torborg was smart, knew baseball, and had been a catcher for the Los Angeles Dodgers when Sandy Koufax and Don Drysdale were two of the most dominating pitchers in the game.

It was Torborg who discovered Nolan was throwing too hard. Nolan thought that's what he needed to do to make his pitches faster. But Torborg explained, "When you rush your motion and you stride out too soon, your arm can't catch up and the ball gets released too soon."

Nolan knew that Torborg was right. Together they

worked on his pitching delivery. They wanted to get his stride and release just right for the fastest possible pitch.

Tom Morgan had some ideas too. He didn't want to change Nolan's delivery, but he did want to make it more compact. Together, they worked to make a more natural, fluid pitching motion that would make Nolan less wild.

Despite an awful spring training, Rice named Nolan as one of his four starting pitchers. He was finally going to get his chance. His military obligation was over. A four-man rotation meant he would start every fourth game. With good coaching, regular starts, and management behind him, Nolan was ready.

His first start came on the third game of the season. It was a home game against the Minnesota Twins. It was a low-scoring pitchers' duel. By the end of the game, Nolan had his first win as an Angel. The score was 2–0. Nolan had struck out 10 batters.

But, as had happened so often in Nolan's career, disaster would soon strike. Nolan went into a slump. By mid-May, he had lost four games and had a 2–4 record. Rice told him the bad news. He had lost his job as a starting pitcher. It was back to the bullpen.

That's when Tom Morgan stepped up to the plate and went to bat for Nolan. He convinced Rice that Nolan would soon be living up to expectations. He promised Rice that he and Torborg would put extra work in with Nolan.

Not since Red Murff had walked up to him as a tenth-grader had anyone in baseball been as important to Nolan as Tom Morgan was that day. Nolan's career was about to take a turn.

When Tom mentioned hard work to Nolan, it was music to his ears. Any kid who got up at 1:00 A.M to deliver newspapers is the kind of kid who wants to work hard. And that's what they did. Pitch after pitch, they worked on the mechanics Nolan needed. It was boring, it was exhausting, and it was slow. But it was making Nolan a better pitcher.

About that same time, Nolan had discovered a forgotten weight room at Anaheim Stadium. It may have been set up by a short-lived professional soccer team and abandoned when their league folded. No one knew for sure. But everyone knew that weights weren't necessary for baseball players and were bad for pitchers.

Nolan wasn't so sure. He looked at the universal gym and began to work out. He also started running.

The more he exercised, the more he liked it. He did bench presses, military presses, leg extensions, and anything else that made him gain strength. He was careful to exercise around his pitching starts. Most of his lifting was done on the first two days after he pitched.

Nolan was also careful not to get caught lifting weights. Baseball teams didn't want their pitchers experimenting with their bodies. But Nolan knew it was helping, so he kept it up.

Nolan's turnaround began almost at once. From 2–4 in mid-May, he was 8–5 by the end of June. Then came July.

On July 1, Nolan won a game at home against the Oakland A's. He struck out 16 batters.

Four days later Nolan took the mound again. The Angels scored only one run for him that day, but it was all Nolan needed. He pitched a complete game shutout, struck out eight, and was the winning pitcher.

Four days later, Nolan took the mound again. This time the opponent was the Boston Red Sox. Nolan began by walking the lead-off batter, centerfielder Tommy Harper. Then he struck out Doug Griffin. Next up was power-hitting Carl Yastrzemski. He singled to left. That was the end for the Red Sox because the rest of the game belonged to Nolan.

Nolan retired the next 26 straight batters. No hits, no walks, no errors. Just outs. When he was finished, he had 16 strikeouts and owned the American League record by striking out eight batters in a row. He even struck out the side on nine pitches. He had done that once before in New York, but now he was the only pitcher who had done it in *both* leagues.

Nolan's reward for his fantastic performances came almost immediately. He was named to the American League All-Star team! Although Nolan didn't play in that All-Star game, he had finally taken his first step toward being a true major league star.

Whenever Nolan's career was going well, disaster would strike. Whether it was an injury, military service, or simply bad pitching, something would derail him. Not this year.

Nolan went on a tear for the second half of the season. In July he struck out 14 Rangers in a 5–0 win. In August he had three straight starts with 10 or more strikeouts. In September he struck out 15 Rangers in one game. His last three games of the season he struck out a total of 39 batters.

Even when Nolan was the losing pitcher, it was lack of offense by his teammates that cost the Angels the game—not poor pitching. When a pitcher goes nine innings and gives up only one or two runs, his team should win. But the Angels were a weak-hitting team. Nolan lost a lot of games where he pitched well but the final score was 1–0 or 2–1.

By the time the season ended, Nolan had established himself as a top pitcher. He had a total of 329 strikeouts—tops in the American League. He also led the league with nine shutouts. His overall record was 19–16 and he had a 2.28 ERA.

Earlier in the season, Nolan had been ready to quit baseball. In May his manager had been ready to demote him to the bullpen. But Nolan had turned it around. It had taken hard work and lots of perseverance. It had taken encouragement from Ruth and help from Tom Morgan and Jeff Torborg. But Nolan had in fact had a great season; he had turned the corner.

If fans thought 1972 was a great season for Nolan, they were in for a big surprise. Next up were the miracle years.

THE MIRACLE YEAR

1973

Aᴏᴛᴇʀ ʜɪs Aʟʟ-Sᴛᴀʀ season in 1972, the Angels nearly doubled Nolan's salary to $54,000. They had confidence in him. The fans had confidence in him. And, most importantly, Nolan had confidence in himself.

Nolan opened the 1973 season with a win against the Royals in Kansas City. He looked sharp with 12 strikeouts in a 3–2 win. He followed that win with an 11-strikeout 4–1 victory over the Twins in front of the home crowd at Anaheim Stadium. A week later he beat the Twins again with a 14-strikeout performance.

But, after racing out to a 3–0 record, Nolan hit a streak of tough luck and won only one while losing three in his next five starts. On May 12 the White Sox knocked him out early, and he left the game with only four strikeouts.

On May 15 the Angels had a Sunday night game with the Kansas City Royals. Since Nolan hadn't pitched much two days earlier, manager Bobby Winkles decided to start Nolan with only two days of rest.

Nolan took his warm-up pitches in the Royals' stadium that night. He looked up in the stands and could tell it was going to be a sparse crowd. That was just as well. Nolan was 4–3 and had bunches of strikeouts, but he knew he had to work his way out of his current slump.

As he warmed up, he could tell his fastball wasn't as fast as usual. He would need to pitch smart tonight —try to avoid walks and bad pitches.

Nolan's California teammates gave him a nice present in the top of the first inning. Vada Pinson singled and Frank Robinson walked. Bob Oliver and Alan Gallagher followed with a pair of RBI singles. The Angels led 2–0.

In the bottom of the first, Nolan walked leadoff hitter Steve Hovley. Walking a leadoff batter is always a bad sign. To make matters worse, Hovley stole second.

No outs and a runner in scoring position at second. Nolan knew what to do. He struck out Fred Patek, he struck out Amos Otis, and he struck out John Mayberry.

Nolan got through the second without giving up any hits or walks. In the third he issued a one-out walk to catcher Carl Taylor but then struck out Patek and got Hovley out on an easy grounder to the mound.

In the California sixth, Bob Oliver hit a solo homer, upping the Angels' lead to 3–0. That's when everyone noticed Nolan was pitching a no-hitter.

Baseball players are superstitious. One of their superstitions involves not talking to a pitcher when he has a chance for a no-hitter. Don't talk to him, don't sit near him, don't do anything to jinx him. By now Nolan was sitting all by himself.

Nolan finished the sixth and seventh innings with his no-hitter intact. He had 11 strikeouts.

He took the mound for the bottom of the eighth. In barely over five years in the majors, Nolan had flirted with no-hitters six times. He had thrown two one-hit games and four two-hitters. Nolan wanted a no-hitter; he wanted it bad.

Nolan quickly got one out. Gail Hopkins came up as a pinch hitter for catcher Carl Taylor. Then it happened. Hopkins got his bat on the ball and hit a lazy line drive to shallow centerfield, a sure hit. But shortstop Rudy Meoli knew what he had to do. He raced after the ball at full speed. With his back to the plate, he made a spectacular over-the-shoulder catch. The no-hitter was alive! Nolan quickly got the next batter out to send the game to the ninth.

A no-hitter is special for any major league pitcher. Most pitchers never do it. Even the greatest no-hit pitcher ever, Sandy Koufax, had done it only four times. Nolan knew all this, but he had to put it out of his mind and concentrate on pitching.

The Angels didn't score in the ninth. Due up for

the Royals was the top of the order: Patek, Hovley, Otis.

Nolan looked into catcher Jeff Torborg for the sign. Fastball. He gripped the ball across the seams and fired it in. It was high but Patek went after it. He hit an easy pop-up to first. One out!

Hovley worked the count to 2–2. Torborg signed for a fastball. Nolan gave it everything he had. Hovley swung. *Thwap!* Hovley had missed. Two outs!

The only thing between Nolan and a no-hitter was Amos Otis sitting 60 feet 6 inches away. Torborg signaled for a fastball. Nolan wound up and delivered it with everything he had. Otis swung. *Thwap!* It was in Torborg's glove. "Strike one."

Nolan took a deep breath. He looked at Torborg. Fastball was the sign; that's all Nolan wanted to pitch anyway.

Nolan gripped the ball in his glove. He found the seams with his fingers. He went into his motion, kicked his leg high, and delivered. *Crack!* Otis smashed a deep flyball to right. Rightfielder Ken Berry took off running. He caught it at the warning track. Three outs! A no-hitter!

His teammates mobbed him. Nolan had done it. He had thrown a major league no-hitter!

The media hoopla began immediately. The national press started doing stories on Nolan, not just about his no-hitter but about his amazing fastball and all those strikeouts.

The Angels promoted him like a star. On the days

he pitched the marquee at the stadium would read *Nolan Ryan v. The Yankees* (or whatever team they were playing).

By now Nolan was enough of a star to have his own nickname. *Von Ryan's Express* had been a hit movie in the 1960s. Sportswriters were always eager for creative nicknames, and the "Ryan" part of the movie title and the speed of Nolan's fastball were a natural connection. The sportswriters began to refer to Nolan as "the Ryan Express."

But media, marquees and nicknames aside, Nolan knew there was a long, tough season ahead. He pitched well for the next two months. But the Angels didn't back him up with many runs. He struck out 10 or more batters six times in games he didn't win. On July 3 he reached a milestone by striking out the 1,000th batter of his career, when he victimized Oakland third baseman Sal Bando. By mid-July, he led the majors in strikeouts but had only a 10–11 record to show for it.

Pitchers with losing records aren't usually named to the All-Star team. In 1973 Nolan was going to be an exception. For the second year in a row, Nolan made the All-Star team.

Despite his losing record, Nolan knew he had good stuff. He was warming up to pitch July 15 in Tiger Stadium in Detroit. As he threw, he felt his fastball was on fire and his curveball was breaking hard. He knew it was going to be a good game.

63

Nolan stopped to say something to Tom Morgan before he went out to pitch the first inning. He told Tom he had great stuff. "If I ever have a chance to pitch another no-hitter, it'll be today."

Art Kusnyer, the Angels' other catcher, was behind the plate that day. The Angels were worried that Detroit was going to try to steal their signs, so Kusnyer and Nolan agreed that Nolan would call the pitches. Nolan would touch the front of his cap for a curveball and the back for a fastball. Kusnyer would then flash some meaningless sign to confuse the Tigers.

Nolan was right about having good stuff that day. His fastball was really sizzling and going right where Nolan wanted it. His curveball was breaking a good foot. By the end of the seventh inning, Nolan had struck out 16 Tigers and had not allowed a hit.

It was in the top of the eighth that the California bats came alive. California, which had a one-run lead, scored five more in the top of the eighth. Pitchers love for their team to score runs, but it was a very long inning. The Angels had given Nolan a six-run lead, but Nolan was stiff and sore from sitting too long in the dugout. He knew he wouldn't have the same velocity on his pitches for the last two innings.

By now, the Tiger fans and dugout were trying to jinx Nolan. Tiger manager Billy Martin kept screaming to Nolan that he was going to lose his no-hitter on the next pitch. But Nolan was in a zone. He totally focused on his next pitch.

Nolan set the Tigers down in order in the bottom

of the eighth. But the stiffness hurt him and he struck out only one batter. Now he was only three outs away from a second no-hitter.

California didn't score in the top of the ninth. Due up for the Tigers were the 2, 3 and 4 batters: center-fielder Mickey Stanley, designated hitter Gates Brown, and clean-up batter Norm Cash.

Nolan signaled a fastball to his catcher. He looked in at Stanley, threw his pitch. "Strike one!"

Nolan signaled for another fastball. He delivered. *Crack!* Stanley smacked a groundball right at shortstop Rudy Meoli. Meoli fielded it cleanly and threw to first. One out!

By now the Tiger fans, all 41,411 of them, had seen enough of Nolan to realize this was something special. They started cheering for him! They wanted to see a no-hitter.

Next up was Gates Brown. Brown was a problem for a pitcher like Nolan because his favorite pitch to hit was a low fastball. That was exactly the type of pitch Nolan usually tried to throw.

Nolan wanted to be very careful with Brown. But he got too careful and was behind in the count. Nolan could have walked Brown and moved on to the next batter, but he decided to go right at him. He touched the back of his cap to signal a fastball! Nolan wound up and delivered. *Crack!* Brown smashed a line drive toward left. Rudy Meoli reacted instinctively and put his glove in the air. *Pop!* He snared the liner just as it went past his head. Two outs!

Clean-up batter Norm Cash came to the plate. He was the only thing standing between Nolan and a no-hitter.

Nolan wanted this no-hitter. He focused on the batter. He was going to get nothing but fastballs. Nolan was going to live or die with his best pitch.

Nolan threw his best heat three times. The count was 1–2. One more strike and the no-hitter was his.

Nolan touched the back of his cap. This was going to be it. He wound up and delivered. *Pop!* It was an easy pop-up to short left. Meoli drifted back and made the catch. Three outs! Nolan had his *second* no-hitter!

After the game the media went wild. Nolan was now a true star—one of the top pitchers in the game.

Nolan's manager, Bobby Winkles, told the newspapers it was "the best game I've ever seen pitched." Catcher Art Kusnyer showed off his bruised fingers and hands as proof of how hard Nolan had been throwing.

Home plate umpire Ron Luciano, who had a close-up view of every pitch, said the batters simply had "no chance."

"When he wanted to hit an inside corner—he hit an inside corner. When he wanted to throw letter-high—he threw letter-high." Luciano said. "It was the most perfect pitching I've ever seen in my life."

Nolan continued to pitch well for the rest of July and through August. He was striking a lot of batters out, but his weak-hitting team wasn't doing much to help his win-loss record. He pitched into extra innings against Baltimore, striking out 13, only to lose the game in the 11th, 3–1.

On August 25 he struck out eight Red Sox in a losing effort where his teammates failed to score any runs. But by that time he had amassed an incredible 304 strikeouts. He joined Sandy Koufax and Rube Waddell as the only three major league pitchers to strike out 300 or more batters in two straight years.

But despite pitching well, Nolan still had a losing record. A 14–16 record left Nolan frustrated. Then an amazing thing happened. Nolan's teammates, who had the worst team batting average in the league, finally started scoring runs for him. In fact, they gave him at least three runs in every game the rest of the season.

Nolan went on a roll. The last 30 days of the season belonged to him.

First up were the dreaded Yankees. Nolan threw a one-hitter, struck out ten, and ended up with a 5–0 shutout win.

Then came the A's. Twelve strikeouts later, Nolan had a 3–1 win.

The White Sox were next. Twelve strikeouts and another 3–1 victory for Nolan.

Now it was the Royals' turn. Ten strikeouts and they, too, fell 3–1. That game tied Nolan with Sandy Koufax for the most games in a season with 10 or more strikeouts at 21.

The Rangers were next. Nolan had only seven strikeouts but won the game 6–2.

By now, Nolan's losing record was erased. He was 19–16. He had two starts left for a chance to win 20 games. Twenty wins was an important milestone for any pitcher. Without 20 wins, Nolan's season wouldn't be complete.

He also had an outside chance at one of the most important records in baseball. The single-season strikeout record stood at 382 and was held, of course, by Sandy Koufax. Even 300 strikeouts in a season would be rare. When Koufax struck out 382 in 1965, people thought that record would last forever. Nolan had 355—he needed 28 strikeouts to break the record.

Nolan's first chance to get 20 wins came on the road against Minnesota. Little did Nolan know it was going to be one of his worst pitching performances of the season.

Minnesota batters hit Nolan's pitches all over the park. He gave up a total of seven runs. Normally, that's a disaster. But the Angels were giving Nolan plenty of run support. This time they gave him 15 runs. Nolan ended up with a complete game victory.

It wasn't pretty, but Nolan had his 20th win. Nolan also had 12 strikeouts. He was just 15 short of tying Koufax's record and 16 short of breaking it.

Nolan wanted that record. His competitive fires were burning.

His last start was scheduled for Thursday, September 28. He hoped if he was close, Winkles would let him pitch some on Sunday, the last day of the season. It would be on only two days' rest after a long, exhausting season, but Nolan had fixed all his attention on getting the record.

Nolan took the mound to begin the game; he wanted 16 strikeouts. The crowd filled Anaheim Stadium; they wanted 16 strikeouts. This was the game that everyone wanted to see.

The Twins had other ideas. Two singles, a double and three runs later, Bobby Winkles was on the mound ready to take Nolan out.

"Are you all right, Nolan?"

"I think so," replied Nolan. "I just haven't gotten loose yet."

"All right, then. Get loose. You've got a lot of pitching to do."

Nolan knew that he had to settle down right away or he'd be out of the game. The next batter was Jim Holt. Nolan struck him out.

Nolan's teammates came through for him in the bottom of the first. They scored three runs to tie the game.

From then on Nolan settled down. After five innings, he had 12 strikeouts.

Nolan didn't get a strikeout in the sixth. He had three innings left. He needed four strikeouts.

In the Twins' seventh, the first three batters were Harmon Killebrew, George Mitterwald, and Steve Brye. Killebrew became Nolan's 380th strikeout victim of the season. Next up was George Mitterwald; he became

381. Brye came to the plate and was 382. Nolan had struck out the side and had tied Sandy Koufax's record.

By the eighth inning the crowd was reacting to every pitch. Every strike brought wild cheers. Every fly-out, pop-out, and ground-out brought groans. The fans didn't care about the outcome of the game; they wanted to see Nolan get the record.

The crowd did a lot of groaning because Nolan didn't get a single strikeout in either the eighth or ninth inning. He didn't give up any runs either. Going into the bottom of the ninth, the score was tied 3–3.

The home crowd rooted against the Angels in the bottom of the ninth. They wanted extra innings. They wanted Nolan to get another chance. The Angels didn't score. The game stayed tied.

The tenth inning came and went. No strikeouts. The score was still tied.

Winkles was concerned about letting Nolan out to pitch the 11th. He told Nolan this was his absolute last inning. What he didn't say, but Nolan knew, was that this was the last chance for the record. After pitching 11 innings, there was no way Nolan could come back to pitch on Sunday. It was now or never.

Nolan was exhausted, but every ounce of his body wanted this record. He just had to do it. He dug deep down inside.

First up was Steve Brye. Nolan got two quick strikes on him. The crowd went crazy. Everyone screamed as Nolan threw his next pitch. Brye swung. There was a moment of absolute breathless quiet. Foul tip, signaled the umpire as the fans finally saw the ball roll behind the catcher.

Still with two strikes, Nolan reared back and fired. Again the crowd screamed. *Pop!* Brye hit an easy pop-up for the first out of the inning. The crowd moaned in unison.

Next up was Rod Carew, the American League's leading hitter. Nolan had already struck Carew out three times. Nolan knew Carew was too good a hitter to want to be struck out a fourth time. Nolan pitched him very carefully and ended up walking him.

Tony Oliva was up next. Nolan got a strike past him, but he flew out on the next pitch. Nolan was down to *one out left* to get strikeout 383.

Rich Reese came to the plate. This was it. Nolan would have the record or not on this batter.

Nolan walked off the pitcher's mound. He took a couple of deep breaths. No curveball, no change-up. This was going to be pure heat. Nolan was exhausted. He had no physical energy left. He was going to pitch with his heart.

Nolan stepped back on the mound. His catcher gave him the fastball sign. Nolan went into his wind-up and delivered. Reese swung and missed. "Strike one!"

Nolan took the sign for another fastball. He went into his wind-up and delivered again. Swing and a miss. "Strike two!"

The whole stadium was on its feet making a deafening roar. They, too, were exhausted, but they screamed all the same. Nolan wound up and delivered. Reese

71

swung and missed. *"Strike three!"* The strikeout record belonged to Nolan!

The crowd went wild. Nolan's teammates charged from the dugout to congratulate him. The fans applauded and cheered as the game had to be temporarily stopped. The entire centerfield scoreboard was lit up with huge numerals "383."

The 1973 season was over. Nolan had pitched two no-hitters, set the single-season strikeout record, and set the single-season record for most 10-or-more strikeout games with 23. He had won 21 games.

Nolan was now the star he always knew he could be. Whitey Herzog, then the Texas Ranger manager, summed it up best. "Nolan Ryan," he said, "has the greatest arm in the history of baseball."

THE MIRACLE
CONTINUES

1974

THE 1974 SEASON BEGAN on a frigid day at Comiskey Park in Chicago. Some 30,000 fans braved 37-degree weather to watch the opening day game featuring White Sox ace Wilbur Wood against the Angels' ace, Nolan Ryan.

Both pitchers struggled in the cold weather. Nolan gave up two runs in the first two innings. Before he left the game after eight innings, Nolan had walked 10 batters and allowed four hits. He had only five strikeouts. But Nolan pitched well enough to hold the White Sox to just those two runs.

Wood also struggled and was taken out for a relief pitcher in the seventh. The Angels' batters got three runs on Wood, but they erupted for five runs in the eighth against the White Sox relief pitchers.

Nolan ended up as the winning pitcher. American League hitters should have hoped for 37-degree temperatures all season long because that was the only thing that cooled Nolan's fastball off that season.

In mid-April, Nolan struck out 11 Twins in a game. The next month he struck out 15 Red Sox. But Nolan was just getting warmed up.

On June 14, Nolan took on the Red Sox at Anaheim Stadium. He ended up pitching 12 innings. By the time Nolan threw the last of his 235 pitches, he had struck out an incredible 19 batters.

The American League record for the most strikeouts in a nine-inning game was 18, held by Bob Feller. The major league record, held by both Steve Carlton and Tom Seaver, was 19 in a nine-inning game. Since Nolan's 19 came in a 12-inning game, he didn't tie or break any of these records. But everyone expected that one day he would.

The wait wasn't long. On August 12, Nolan faced the Red Sox again. The hometown Angel fans watched in amazement as Nolan struck out Red Sox batters all game long. Starting with Cecil Cooper and ending with Bernie Carbo, Nolan fanned 19 batters on the way to a 4–2 victory. Nolan had broken Bob Feller's American League record and tied Tom Seaver and Steve Carlton's major league record.

Tom Seaver, Nolan's old New York teammate, was still the ace of the Mets' pitching staff. He telephoned Nolan after the game to congratulate him.

But if American League batters were hoping Nolan

would let up, they were wrong. Eight days later, Nolan pitched against Detroit. This time he went 11 innings, and he again ended up with 19 strikeouts.

Nineteen-strikeout games are rare feats. Yet Nolan had an incredible *three* in one season. The record of 19 in a nine-inning game that he shared with Seaver and Carlton lasted 12 more years. It was finally broken when Boston Red Sox ace Roger Clemens struck out 20.

The Angels were struggling as a team in 1974. Nolan was pitching great baseball. He was winning games and setting records. But fan interest in a last-place team was steadily declining.

The Angels' public relations director, George Lederer, promoted Nolan as a way to get more fans into the ballpark. But by the second half of the '74 season, the Angels were so bad they had become the object of jokes. Lederer needed something to get fans to watch games.

He finally came up with an idea. The fastest pitch ever recorded had been thrown by Bob Feller in 1946. It had been recorded by the Army. The official speed was 98.6 mph.

Lederer contacted scientists at Rockwell International. Dick Brandewie came up with a way to measure a pitch's speed by shooting an infrared light beam from the press box down to home plate.

Lederer promoted the event not just as a chance to record the speed of a Nolan Ryan fastball but as a contest. Fans could send in a postcard guessing what Nolan's fastest pitch would be. The fan with the closest guess would win a trip to Hawaii.

Nolan's fastballs were measured in the August 20 game with the Tigers and a September 7 game with the White Sox. Brandewie announced the results during the September 7 game over the public address system. Nolan had thrown two pitches against the Tigers at 100.9 mph and one against the White Sox at 100.8 mph.

Nolan now officially owned the record for the fastest pitch ever scientifically measured. The record was recognized in the *Guinness Book of World Records* as the fastest pitch ever thrown.

In many ways 1974 was a repeat of 1973. Nolan pitched well. He struck out a lot of batters. The big difference was that Nolan had not pitched a no-hitter.

On June 27, Nolan came close when he pitched a one-hitter against Texas. Then, on August 7, Nolan went into the ninth inning with a no-hitter against the White Sox. With one out, first baseman Dick Allen hit a slow rolling infield ground ball. He was safe at first with an infield single.

By early September, Nolan was frustrated. He had pitched well all season long, but his record was only 17–16. But just like the year before, September belonged to Nolan.

First up were the Chicago White Sox at Anaheim

Stadium. Nolan pitched a complete game, struck out nine, and won 3–1.

Next, the Kansas City Royals came to town. Nolan's fastball blazed, his curveball broke hard, and 15 Royals struck out. Nolan won 3–2.

Then came a road game against Chicago. Seven strikeouts later, Nolan had his 20th win of the season with a 6–2 victory.

Next it was the Royals in Kansas City. Nolan struck out nine in a 9–3 win.

Nolan's last start of the 1974 season came on September 28. Although he had an incredible 352 strikeouts, he couldn't possibly break his record of 383. The Angels were hopelessly in last place with the worst record in the American League. All Nolan could hope to do was pitch his best, give the fans their money's worth, and perhaps win his 22nd game of the season.

The opponents that day, the Minnesota Twins, were the best hitting team in the American League. Their star sluggers were Rod Carew, Larry Hisle, and Tony Oliva. Nolan knew he had to pitch well against heavy hitters like that.

Only 10,000 fans made it out to the park that day. Nolan felt good in warm-ups. He decided to try his heat out on the first batter, centerfielder Steve Brye.

He wound up and delivered. *Thwap!* "Strike one."

His next pitch was the same. "Strike two."

Pitch number three. "Strike three." Brye sat down.

Rod Carew followed. Again Nolan threw three straight strikes. Carew sat down.

77

Bobby Darwin came next. He, too, struck out.

The second inning went the same. Nolan faced three batters and struck them all out.

Nolan talked to his catcher, Tom Egan. They both knew Nolan's fastball was really popping. Nolan decided he'd just let it all hang out.

Perhaps Nolan relaxed too much. He walked seven batters in the next three innings. But he didn't give up any hits or runs. His teammates came through with two runs in the third and two more in the fourth.

By the sixth inning, Nolan had a 4–0 lead and his no-hitter intact. His fastball was on fire and his curveball unhittable.

At this point, Nolan reached inside himself. He wanted a no-hitter. He wasn't going to fool around with any more walks. It was time to get batters out.

In the sixth he got three straight outs, striking out two. In the seventh he again got three straight outs but without a strikeout. In the eighth, three straight outs, again striking out two.

He went into the ninth facing designated hitter Tony Oliva, leftfielder Larry Hisle, and first baseman Pat Bourque.

Oliva made a quick out. Nolan had been in the same position just a month earlier. One out in the ninth, with a no-hitter going. He was determined not to lose it again.

He bore down on Hisle and struck him out. His 14th strikeout victim of the game. One out to go.

Harmon Killebrew came to the plate to pinch hit

for Bourque. Killebrew was a heavy hitter. Nolan pitched carefully. He ended up walking him.

Next up was shortstop Eric Soderholm. Soderholm worked the count to 2–2. Nolan didn't want to walk Soderholm. He also didn't want to give him a pitch to hit.

Nolan looked at Egan for the sign. Could he end it with this pitch? He checked the runner at first, then delivered. *Thwap!* The pitch was high, but Soderholm's swing missed.

Nolan had done it. A *third* no-hitter!

He was now tied for second in career no-hitters with Larry Corcoran of the Cubs, Jim Maloney of the Reds, and Bob Feller of the Cleveland Indians. Only Sandy Koufax, with four, had thrown more.

Nolan finished the '74 season with a 22–16 record. For the third straight year, he led the American League in strikeouts. Who could guess what he might be able to do in the future? As far as Nolan and baseball fans were concerned, 1975 couldn't start soon enough.

GOOD TIMES,
BAD TIMES

SUNDAY AFTERNOON, JUNE 1, 1975. Eighteen thousand Angel fans came out to enjoy an afternoon of baseball. Their ace, Nolan Ryan, was taking on the always heavy-hitting Baltimore Orioles. It figured to be a good game —power pitching against power hitting.

Nolan was a fan favorite in Anaheim. He had given the fans three exciting years. But 1975 had started off as Nolan's best year yet. He was leading the majors in strikeouts and had an 8–3 record.

While the fans waited for the game to begin, a Nolan Ryan they knew very little about was taking his warm-up tosses. Nolan had many things on his mind.

First, his secret weight training and conditioning were really paying off. Nolan had been right—pitchers really could benefit from conditioning. By now, Nolan had a universal gym at home and was perfecting his weight program every day, even in the off-season. This was allowing Nolan to not only pitch lots of innings but to actually get stronger as the game went on. Instead of tiring like other pitchers, Nolan's fastest pitches came in the late innings.

Second, all of his hard work with pitching coach Tom Morgan and his teammates was also paying off. With the Mets, Nolan had been a one-pitch pitcher. He lived or died with his fastball. With the Angels he had developed a deadly curve. Now he was finally getting his change-up to work.

A good change-up should be 10-15 mph slower than a pitcher's fastball. Nolan always wanted to throw it too fast, which made his change-up just a slower version of his fastball. But a change-up needs to fool a batter. To do that, it needs to look exactly like a fastball, but a full 10-15 mph slower. Nolan was finally getting it right.

But with his conditioning and pitching getting better, Nolan also knew there was a dark cloud on the horizon. His pitching arm was in constant pain whenever he wasn't throwing. It was hurting so badly that Nolan could barely brush his teeth or comb his hair. Once he loosened up and threw hard, the pain wasn't as bad. But Nolan knew that trouble couldn't be too far away.

It was with these thoughts that Nolan took the mound. He was doing what he loved to do—to pitch. He was ready to take it to the Orioles.

Nolan held the Orioles hitless through the first three innings. With two out in the bottom of the third, his teammates came up with three straight singles and scored one run.

By the seventh inning, Nolan still had a no-hitter going. The fans stayed standing and began cheering on every pitch.

Nolan, however, knew it was too early to begin getting serious about a no-hitter. Yes, he had pitched three, but he had also gone to the seventh inning with a no-hitter 10 times and not made it. He was more concerned about having only a one-run lead.

Nolan put the pain in his arm and the tremendous excitement of the fans behind him. He had to concentrate on getting outs.

By the top of the ninth, Nolan's no-hitter was intact. He was just three outs away from a record-tying fourth no-hitter.

Superstar athletes like Nolan Ryan have a lot of talent and they work very hard to develop it. But they also have something else. Call it competitive spirit or drive, but it's really something extra—something that separates them from mere stars. They simply want it more than any other human being. That day, Nolan really wanted a fourth no-hitter.

Due up for the Orioles in the top of the ninth were the 3, 4 and 5 hitters. Leftfielder Al Bumbry, designated hitter Tommie Davis, and second baseman Bobby Grich. Davis and Grich were the toughest outs in the Orioles' line-up.

Nolan went to work. He got Bumbry to fly out to left. One out. Davis grounded out to second. Two outs.

It was down to Bobby Grich. As Grich came up, the crowd began to get louder. They had been on their feet for the last three innings, and they were emotionally coming to a peak.

Nolan checked his catcher Elly Rodriguez for the sign. Curveball. Nolan fingered the seams of the ball in his glove for his curveball grip. He went into his wind-up, then delivered. "Strike one!"

He checked the sign again. Fastball. His fingers gripped the ball across the seams. Wind-up. Delivery. *Thwap!* He hit Rodriguez' glove just off the inside corner. "Ball!"

He checked Rodriguez' sign again. Curveball. Nolan threw it. "Strike two!"

Nolan checked for the sign. Fastball. Enough curveballs. Nolan wanted to throw his heat. He gripped the ball, wound up, and delivered. Grich swung. "Foul ball!" The count stayed 1–2.

Rodriguez signaled for another fastball. Nolan wound up and delivered. *Thwap!* For a second the crowd was silent. "Ball," signaled the umpire. Just outside. The count was 2–2.

By now the crowd was in a frenzy. The noise was deafening. Rodriguez gave Nolan the sign for another fastball. Nolan wound up and delivered. Grich swung. "Foul ball."

The crowd went beyond frenzy. They wanted the no-hitter! They were screaming for it.

Nolan made a slight move with his teeth and lips. It was a special signal to his catcher that he wanted to throw a change-up. No one in the stadium saw the sign except Rodriguez. He flashed a quick sign to Nolan to let him know he had seen it.

Nolan Ryan, the Ryan Express, the king of fastballs, the fastest pitcher ever was going to try for a no-hitter with a change-up? Not a single fan would have believed it. Neither would Bobby Grich.

Nolan wound up and delivered. Grich was fooled completely. He watched the pitch go by. "Strike three!"

Nolan had done it again! The *fourth* no-hitter was his!

The fans went wild. The media went wild. Nolan had tied Koufax for most career no-hitters. He had four no-hitters in barely a two-year span!

To Nolan this was more than just an incredible fourth no-hitter. He had proved to himself that he was a complete pitcher. Always before, he had relied on his fastball. But against Grich he had put it all on the line with his change-up. Nolan had been a thrower in high school, the minors, and with the Mets. A very talented thrower but a thrower nonetheless. Now he was a pitcher—one of the best pitchers in the game.

As if to confirm his status, Sandy Koufax sent Nolan a telegram congratulating him on tying his no-hitter record. Sandy had also sent his congratulations when Nolan broke the single-season strikeout record. For a kid who had sat as a fan in Colt Stadium watching Koufax pitch, this had a special meaning for Nolan.

But it was one of Nolan's other childhood idols who was soon to intersect with Nolan's career on the playing field. Next up were the Milwaukee Brewers and Hank Aaron.

Thirty thousand fans and the national media descended upon Anaheim Stadium. They wanted to see if Nolan could pitch back-to-back no-hitters. That had been done only once, when Johnny Vander Meer of the Cincinnati Reds did it in 1938.

Once again Nolan brought a no-hitter into the late innings. By the fifth inning, the fans were cheering on every pitch. With two outs in the sixth, Hank Aaron came to the plate. Aaron smacked a clean single up the middle. That ended the no-hitter.

Nolan continued with a great pitching performance. He finished with a two-hit shutout. His season record stood at 10–3. He was on top of the mountain.

The crash came very quickly. There were four pieces of calcium rubbing the joint inside his elbow. That was the cause of his pain and stiffness. Even Nolan's hard work and drive were no match for those little calcium chips.

Nolan went into a tailspin. Although his record was still good enough to be named to his third All-Star team, his pitching effectiveness was over. He won four more games while losing nine. At one point he lost eight straight. Nolan couldn't pitch with the pain. His 1975 season ended with an elbow operation in August. His final record was 14–12.

During the off-season, Nolan and Ruth's second son was born. They named him Reese after Nolan's coach and mentor, Jimmy Reese.

Despite his elbow pain, Nolan was thriving with the Angels. His baseball career was fantastic, his family was growing, and southern California fit Nolan well. He had never gotten used to life with the Mets or New York City. He and Ruth had rented an apartment in Queens while living in New York. To a country boy this was an unfamiliar world of heavy traffic, constant crowds, and bagels and lox. In fact, his favorite activity in New York City was finding a city park to take his black lab Molly out for a good run.

In California Nolan enjoyed the support of Angels' owner Gene Autry. Autry had made a fortune as a cowboy film star. He and Nolan had plenty in common and were good friends.

The 1976 season was really two seasons for Nolan. Coming back from his elbow surgery, he got off to a terrible start. By midseason, he had a 6–9 record with a too high ERA of 3.84.

The second half of the season, Nolan began to return to his top playing form. He was 11–9 with a 2.98 ERA. When the season was over, Nolan led the league in strikeouts, with 327, and shutouts, with 7.

The real highlight of the season came on August 31, while Nolan was pitching against the Tigers at Anaheim Stadium. Nolan won the game 6–3 while striking out 11. The first strikeout, against Ron LeFlore, was the 2,000th of Nolan's career.

Even as a baby,
Nolan had his right
hand ready to throw.
All he needed was a
baseball.
—Courtesy Ruth Ryan

Nolan getting ready to go
to school.
—Courtesy Ruth Ryan

Nolan has always been a Texan through and through.
—Courtesy Ruth Ryan

Nolan made All-Stars still using his Nocona glove. The glove is on display at the Nolan Ryan Exhibit in Alvin.
—Courtesy Ruth Ryan

*One of Nolan's minor league stops was with the
Jacksonville Suns.*

—Courtesy Ruth Ryan

As a new talent with the Mets, Nolan was a scary sight for batters.

—Courtesy Ruth Ryan

*Nolan with Tom Seaver—two Hall of Famers
in their early days.*

—Courtesy Ruth Ryan

Nolan became a dominating pitcher with the Angels. Here he pitched his first no-hitter on May 15, 1973, against Kansas City.

—Courtesy Ruth Ryan

Nolan with cowboy movie star and Angels owner Gene Autry.

Nolan set the single-season strikeout record with 383 on
September 27, 1973.

—Courtesy Ruth Ryan

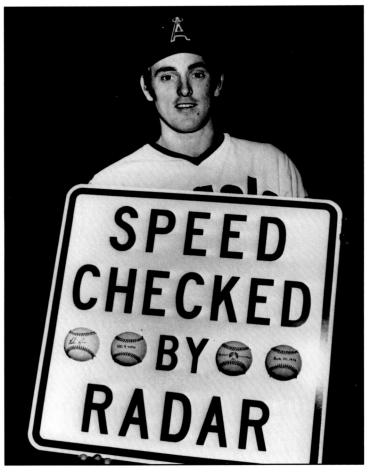

*Rockwell International scientists measured Nolan's fastball
at 100.9 mph—the fastest pitch ever
scientifically measured.*

—Courtesy Baseball Hall of Fame Library,
Cooperstown, NY

Reid and Reese visit their father's dugout.
—Courtesy Ruth Ryan

As a Texas Ranger, Nolan, who was more than 40 years old, racked up his 5,000th strikeout, 300th win, and pitched his sixth and seventh no-hitters.

—Courtesy Texas Rangers

*The 300th win came on July 31, 1990, in an 11-3 victory
over Milwaukee.*

—Courtesy Texas Rangers

Nolan and Ruth visit President and Mrs. George Bush
at the White House. Bush was captain of his
college baseball team at Yale.
—Courtesy George Bush Presidential Library

Baseball commissioner Bud Selig and Hall of Fame President
Ed Stack present Nolan his plaque on July 25, 1999.
—Courtesy Baseball Hall of Fame Library,
Milo Stewart, Jr., Cooperstown, NY

The Ryan family during the Hall of Fame weekend, 1999. From left: Reid and wife Nicole, Ruth, Nolan, Wendy, Reese's wife Alison, and Reese.

—Courtesy Baseball Hall of Fame Library,
Milo Stewart, Jr., Cooperstown, NY

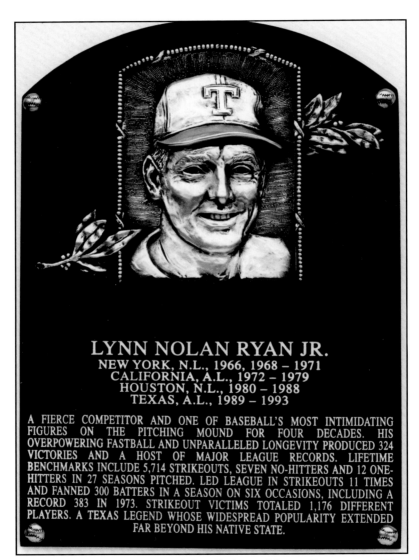

LYNN NOLAN RYAN JR.

NEW YORK, N.L., 1966, 1968 – 1971
CALIFORNIA, A.L., 1972 – 1979
HOUSTON, N.L., 1980 – 1988
TEXAS, A.L., 1989 – 1993

A FIERCE COMPETITOR AND ONE OF BASEBALL'S MOST INTIMIDATING FIGURES ON THE PITCHING MOUND FOR FOUR DECADES. HIS OVERPOWERING FASTBALL AND UNPARALLELED LONGEVITY PRODUCED 324 VICTORIES AND A HOST OF MAJOR LEAGUE RECORDS. LIFETIME BENCHMARKS INCLUDE 5,714 STRIKEOUTS, SEVEN NO-HITTERS AND 12 ONE-HITTERS IN 27 SEASONS PITCHED. LED LEAGUE IN STRIKEOUTS 11 TIMES AND FANNED 300 BATTERS IN A SEASON ON SIX OCCASIONS, INCLUDING A RECORD 383 IN 1973. STRIKEOUT VICTIMS TOTALED 1,176 DIFFERENT PLAYERS. A TEXAS LEGEND WHOSE WIDESPREAD POPULARITY EXTENDED FAR BEYOND HIS NATIVE STATE.

—Courtesy Baseball Hall of Fame Library, Cooperstown, NY

It was during 1977 spring training that the Ryans' daughter, Wendy, was born. Up until then, the Ryans had lived in a rental house in California and returned home to Alvin in the off-season. Now they bought a home in Villa Park. With their oldest son Reid getting into school age, it was time to have more permanent roots in southern California.

The Angels were determined to be a pennant contender in 1977. They signed Nolan to a new three-year contract. They then brought in three proven hitters—Joe Rudi, Bobby Grich, and Don Baylor—to bolster their weak hitting line-up.

Nolan pitched well throughout the 1977 season. He finished with a 19–16 record and led the league in strikeouts with 341. He also allowed the fewest hits per innings pitched and posted his second lowest ERA at 2.77. His excellent year was capped off when *The Sporting News* named him American League Pitcher of the Year.

But while Nolan was pitching well, the Angels' new sluggers didn't produce. The team never clicked as a unit, and the Angels finished in fifth place, 28 games behind Kansas City.

Nolan turned 31 in the off-season. At that age many players—especially power pitchers—can expect to begin to decline. The years of tough, physical baseball begin to take a toll on their bodies.

To many it looked like Nolan's decline came in 1978. He pulled a muscle in June. It cost him 21 days on the disabled list. He also missed time with a rib injury in August. The injuries kept Nolan from developing the consistency he needed. He ended up with a frustrating 10–13 record, the worst since his last year with the Mets.

But even in a frustrating year, Nolan's strikeouts continued. With 260, he once again led the American League. One of those strikeouts, against Buddy Bell of the Indians on May 12, was Nolan's career number 2,500.

Baseball, more than any other game, is a game of records. Nolan already owned some of the most important pitching records: the single-season strikeout record and the career no-hitter record. The career strikeout record was another matter entirely. It was owned by Hall of Fame legend Walter Johnson. Johnson had 416 career victories, second only to Cy Young's 511. Johnson's career strikeout total was 3,508, set in 1927. It had already stood for 51 years. Now Nolan, if he could stay healthy for four or five more seasons, had a real shot at that record.

The 1979 season began with a lot of hope for the Angels. They had traded for Rod Carew. From the time he was named 1967 Rookie of the Year, Rod had been one of the best hitters in baseball. Perhaps he could be the key to finally turning the Angels around.

For Nolan, Carew was a great addition to the team. They were both quiet men who loved baseball but after the game wanted to be home with their families. The

Carews—Rod, Marilyn, and their kids—moved into the same block as the Ryans. The two stars were neighbors.

The only bad sign for the 1979 season was that Nolan's contract would expire at the end of the season. Nolan wanted to get a contract extension so he could concentrate on baseball. But general manager Buzzie Bavasi, who had replaced Harry Dalton, would not even discuss it. He told Nolan to wait until after the season. Nolan and Bavasi never developed a friendship like Nolan had with Dalton. Nolan didn't feel that Bavasi supported him the way Dalton did. Nolan decided this would be his last season with the Angels.

Nolan got off to a good start. He was winning ballgames and striking batters out. The Angels were finally winning games and contending for a pennant. Things were going well.

On the homefront, a new Ryan was just beginning his baseball career. Reid, now seven, was in the Little League in Villa Park. On May 9, Reid had just gotten a brand new T-ball uniform. Reid was proud of it. He wanted to show it off.

His mother and Marilyn Carew were talking to each other as they watched the younger kids. Reid, after showing off his uniform to them, ran across the street to show it to the kids.

A few of the kids thought Reid's uniform wasn't all that cool. They told him they were going to rip it up. Reid panicked. He started running across the street back home.

It is every parent's nightmare. Ruth heard the

squealing tires, the thud of the impact. She ran to Reid. "My leg! My leg! Mama, I'm going to die!" he screamed.

One neighbor called an ambulance. Another got a blanket. Ruth knelt beside her son.

Reid was scratched up—his face, arms, and legs. His left leg, the upper bone called the femur, was broken. Ruth could see the broken bone pressing against the skin although it didn't break through.

At the hospital, the doctors took care of the broken leg. But Reid was in too much pain not to have some more serious injury. They were going to have to run tests and maybe do surgery.

Nolan was in Boston at Fenway Park. He wasn't scheduled to pitch. But even when not playing, players could never be interrupted during a game.

Ruth called anyway. Despite the rules, Ruth's voice wasn't taking no for an answer. She got through to Nolan in the bullpen.

Nolan did what any father would do. He changed clothes and drove straight to the airport. Had he checked the airline schedule, he would have found that no plane could take him to Los Angeles that late. But it made no difference. Nolan had to get to his family as soon as possible. He spent the night in the airport and took an early morning flight.

When he arrived at Children's Hospital, Reid was scheduled for exploratory surgery. As Nolan and Ruth kissed Reid, he was wheeled into the operating room. All his parents could do was wait and pray.

The surgeons discovered Reid's spleen was badly

damaged. It had to be removed. One of his kidneys had to be fixed also. The surgery lasted for a while, but finally a groggy Reid was brought out. At least for now the surgery succeeded.

But Reid's problems continued. Two weeks later he was back in surgery. The repaired kidney had to be removed. It's possible to survive with only one kidney and no spleen. Reid was going to have to.

Reid spent the next two months in the hospital. Ruth and Nolan took turns. Except for his nighttime sleep hours, one of them was with Reid the whole time.

As for baseball, Gene Autry made it clear that Nolan's family came first. Nolan could skip road trips, miss starts, and not be with the team except when he was actually pitching.

It was a tough two months for the Ryans. But Nolan also saw other kids who were seriously ill—some who would never go home. Whenever a parent asked Nolan, he would visit with their child, sign an autograph, and offer encouragement. It wasn't something natural for a quiet country boy like Nolan, but he knew what those parents and kids were going through. Nolan believed in helping kids.

Even when Reid finally went home, he was far from healthy. He was in a body cast from the chest down. But Reid did come home, and he did recover.

Despite the tragedy with Reid, Nolan continued to pitch well. He not only was named to his fourth All-

91

Star team, but he was the American League starting pitcher. When the season was over he had a 16–14 record, and for the seventh time in eight years he led the league in strikeouts.

And at long last the Angels won their division! It had been a long, losing struggle for the Angels, but they finally did it. Their glory year ended quickly, however, as Baltimore won the League Championship Series and went on to the World Series.

Nolan had had eight great years with the Angels. He had gone from a talented but raw pitcher with the Mets to one of the top pitchers in the game. Along the way he had added his name to the record books and given the fans some great moments.

Nolan really loved the Angels' fans. They had stuck with them during some tough years. He also liked owner Gene Autry. But he didn't want to play for a team with Buzzie Bavasi as general manager. Bavasi could have signed Nolan for $400,000 per year and a signing bonus of $200,000. That would have made Nolan happy and kept him an Angel. But Nolan knew it was too late now. His time with the Angels was over.

Free agents were getting big bucks during the winter of 1979. But no free agent drew more interest than Nolan. George Steinbrenner of the Yankees made it clear that he would pay any salary Nolan wanted, even a million dollars a year.

Nolan wasn't interested in getting into a bidding war. The Astros were interested in him. Nolan couldn't imagine anything better than pitching for Houston. The

Astrodome was such a short drive from his house in Alvin. He'd be back home in Texas. That's what Nolan really wanted.

Houston wanted Nolan just as badly. They knew what Steinbrenner was offering and could imagine he would go even higher.

Nolan and Houston agreed. He would be an Astro. The contract was for three years at $1 million per year. At that time it was the highest-paying contract in team sports history. Nolan was now the million-dollar man.

MILLION-DOLLAR
MAN

1980–1982

THE 1980 ASTROS HAD plenty of promise. To begin with, J. R. Richard had led the National League in strikeouts in 1979. He was joining Nolan, who had led the American League in strikeouts in 1979. That made a pretty good start for any pitching staff.

The team also had some rising stars like Jose Cruz, Cesar Cedeno, and Joe Morgan. Bill Virdon provided a steady hand as manager. Since Virdon had coached Nolan at Williamsport and Jacksonville, he made Nolan comfortable from the start.

But what Nolan really liked was being home. Not only was the drive short from Alvin to the Dome, but there also was a lot of satisfaction for Nolan. After all, as a fan he had sat in the stadium watching with awe as Sandy Koufax worked on records Nolan now owned.

As a major leaguer, Nolan's first two starts—one a disaster in 1966 and his first career win two years later—had happened in the Dome.

The people of Alvin were thrilled to have Nolan back. They threw a "Welcome Back to Texas Day" in his honor.

There was a lot of controversy about the size of his $1 million contract. But Nolan knew that would be coming, and he handled it as well as possible.

The 1980 season was a dog fight between the Astros and the Dodgers for first place in the National League West. They battled all year long and ended up the season tied. The Astros came out ahead in a one-game playoff to win the title.

But while the Astros succeeded, Nolan had a tough year. He was trying to get used to National League hitters he didn't know. He also had to get used to the National League strike zone. Umpires are supposed to have the same strike zone in both leagues. But National League umpires don't call a high strike. Nolan figured the strike zone was about 25 percent smaller.

By midseason Nolan had a 5–5 record. He was closing in on one career milestone. On July 4 he struck out the Reds' Cesar Geronimo for his 3,000th career K.

At the end of July, the Astros suffered a tough loss when J. R. Richard had a stroke. He missed the rest of the season and never returned as an effective pitcher.

The second half of Nolan's season was only slightly better than the first. He finished 11–10 with 200 strikeouts. Good—but not great.

Despite the tragic loss of Richard, and a loss to Philadelphia in the League Championship Series, it was a good season for the Astros. They had plenty of hope for the future. Part of that hope was that Nolan would pitch like a million-dollar man in 1981.

Nolan indeed was like a new man in 1981. He had figured out the strike zone and knew the hitters. The only thing that could stop him was the two-month players' strike during June and July.

When the strike was over, baseball resumed with the All-Star game. Nolan had pitched well enough before the strike that he was named to his fifth All-Star team—the first time as a National Leaguer. The game was played in Cleveland. Nolan pitched one hitless inning and struck out one batter.

The second half of the season began with a decision that the four teams that were ahead in the divisional standings when the strike started would be declared the first-half winner. If another team won the second half, the two teams would meet in a playoff to determine who would advance.

This was great news for the first-place Dodgers but bad news for the Astros. There was nothing the Astros could do but try to win the second half.

Nolan continued to pitch well. His ERA was his lowest ever. But he was finishing fewer games. Now at 34 years old, he developed a reputation as a pitcher who could be effective for only seven innings. Twice that year he lost no-hitters in the seventh. Even Nolan doubted he could ever pitch another no-hitter.

The Astros–Dodger dog fight continued in the second half. By late September the Astros had a slim lead when the Dodgers came to town.

Nolan was the starting pitcher for the Saturday game. Because of its importance, it was broadcast nationwide on NBC-TV. There were 33,000 fans, including Nolan's mother, on hand to watch the game.

Nolan took the mound to throw his warm-up tosses. He had never had much luck with the Dodgers. For his career he was 1–8 against Los Angeles. His only win was as a Met back in 1968. Nolan put that depressing thought out of his mind. This was 1981 and he had a game to win.

The Astros were decked out in their bright orange rainbow uniforms. They had orange caps with "H" on the front.

Nolan pitched a good first inning, sitting down the Dodgers in order. He was off to a good start.

In the second, Nolan ran into trouble. He issued a lead-off walk to Steve Garvey. Walks are bad, but lead-off walks are worse. Garvey then stole second and went to third on a wild pitch. But Nolan settled down and retired the side again.

Nolan continued to struggle in the third. He again issued a lead-off walk. A second walk that inning put Dodgers on first and second. Nolan pitched his way out of that jam too. Still, his control was off and he knew he needed to pitch better if he was going to win.

The Astros' bats came alive in the bottom of the third. Catcher Alan Ashby stroked a two-run single. The Astros led 2–0.

With that lead, Nolan came out to pitch with more confidence. His curveball got better and his fastball got faster. He found a groove. The Dodgers went three-up, three-down in the fourth. Same in the fifth. Same in the sixth.

The crowd was thinking "no-hitter." The Astro players starting leaving Nolan all alone on the orange bench in the dugout. Nolan, however, just wanted to win. The dreaded seventh inning was coming up—the inning that had already cost him two no-hitters that season.

Steve Garvey was first up. Nolan got him out on a grounder to second. Pedro Guerrero was next. He grounded out to short.

Catcher Mike Scioscia was next. Nolan fell behind in the count. He knew he needed to get his fastball over for a strike. That's exactly what Scioscia figured too. He smacked it deep to right center. It started falling rapidly as it neared the warning path.

Rightfielder Terry Puhl had a good jump on it. He caught up to it while running at full speed. Just as the ball was dropping, Puhl reached out his glove and snared it waist-high. Puhl had kept the no-hitter intact!

Now Nolan believed he had a chance. He knew every no-hitter required at least one great defensive play. Puhl had just given him a gem.

When Nolan went out for the eighth, the fans were

cheering every pitch. Nolan was working off his nervous energy with a big wad of bubble gum. He was even blowing bubbles. But he was all business with his pitches. Once again, the Dodgers went down—1, 2, 3. Nolan had now retired 16 straight Dodgers.

In the Houston eighth, Craig Reynolds hit an RBI double to make the score 3–0. Nolan was the next batter. The crowd gave him a standing ovation.

Nolan's job was to lay down a sacrifice bunt to move Reynolds to third. He got the bat on the ball and sent it down the first base line. Steve Garvey fielded it and tagged Nolan out, but the sacrifice worked as Reynolds moved up to third. He later scored on a Phil Garner single. The Astros then added another run. Nolan now had a 5–0 lead going into the ninth.

In the ninth, Reggie Smith was announced as the pinch hitter for Davey Lopes. Smith, a switch hitter, batted from the left side against Nolan.

Ashby gave Nolan the sign for a fastball. Nolan wound up and delivered. Smith swung and missed. "Strike one!" The crowd was cheering wildly on every pitch.

Nolan wound up and delivered another fastball. Smith swung and missed. "Strike two!"

Nolan decided to go right after Smith. He was going to try to get another fastball in the strike zone. He wound up and delivered. Smith swung again and missed. "Strike three!" One out!

Centerfielder Ken Landreaux was next. He worked the count to 3–1, then hit a routine ground-out to second. Two outs!

Dusty Baker was up next. He was batting .319—third best in the National League. If Nolan wanted a fifth no-hitter, he was going to have to go against one of the best.

The crowd was on its feet, cheering wildly.

Nolan threw a fastball that was high and inside. Baker took it. "Ball one."

Nolan came back with a curveball. It was outside in the dirt. "Ball two."

Nolan looked at Ashby for the sign. He shook him off. He wanted to throw a curve. He gripped the ball, wound up, and delivered.

Baker swung and made contact. He hit a hard grounder to third. Art Howe came up with it cleanly and fired to Denny Walling at first. Three outs!

Nolan had done it! At age 34, he had thrown a record *fifth* no-hitter!

The Astrodome scoreboard erupted in fireworks and rampaging bulls. The fans went wild. The Astros ran onto the field and carried Nolan off on their shoulders. The million-dollar man had proven his worth!

The Astros went on to win the second-half title. They were in a best-of-five playoff with the Dodgers.

Nolan was matched against Dodger ace Fernando Valenzuela in the first game of the series. They both pitched excellent games. The Astros won 3–1 on a two-run homer by Alan Ashby in the bottom of the ninth. Nolan got the win by pitching a two-hitter. He struck out seven. The lone Dodger run came on a Steve Garvey homer off Nolan.

The Astros also took the second game. The series then moved from Houston to Los Angeles for the final three games. Houston needed to win only one. The Dodgers won the next two.

Nolan was matched against Jerry Reuss for the fifth and deciding game. Nolan pitched well for six innings. He gave up two earned runs, and the Dodgers also got one unearned run on some poor Astro fielding. But the Dodgers seemed to have the Astros jinxed. The Astros didn't score a single run and lost the game 4–0.

Losing in the playoffs was disappointing. But Nolan had still had a great year. His final record was 11–5. He also led the National League with an incredibly low 1.69 ERA.

One bonus for Nolan being with the Astros was Gene Coleman. Gene was the Astros' strength and conditioning coach and a professor at the University of Houston at Clear Lake. Hooking up with Gene was the most important thing that happened to Nolan's career since Tom Morgan had talked the Angels into letting Nolan remain a starting pitcher back in his first year with California.

Nolan had developed his weight training program on a hit-or-miss basis. He had to keep it fairly quiet, almost secret.

Gene, however, placed all the Astros in a strength and conditioning program. The Astros had a complete Nautilus set-up with 20 machines. Together, Nolan and

Gene worked out training methods for a power pitcher like Nolan. These training methods were designed to prevent injuries and ended up extending Nolan's career long past the normal fastball pitcher's time in the big leagues.

Gene and Nolan both knew that the power for a fastball comes from the legs, not the arm. The trick is to use the arm to apply the force generated by the legs. But now they wanted to concentrate on Nolan's stomach muscles. If these abdominal muscles were stronger, there would be less stress on Nolan's arm as the force transferred from his legs to his arm.

Nolan loved to work hard. With Gene's help, they developed a conditioning program that worked well for Nolan.

Most fastball pitchers are lucky to still be pitching in their mid-thirties. When Nolan came to the Astros he was 33. Baseball experts expected him to pitch no more than another three or four years. Wrong.

No one knew for sure if all the weight training would pay off. But pay off it did. At 33, Nolan's major league career wasn't even half over. Some of his best years were yet to come. He was now ready to zero in on the Walter Johnson all-time career strikeout record.

AN "UNBREAKABLE"
RECORD

1983–1988

W<small>ALTER</small> "T<small>HE</small> B<small>IG</small> T<small>RAIN</small>" Johnson had pitched for the Washington Senators. His career lasted from 1906 to 1927. When it was done he had 416 career wins, second only to Cy Young's 511 wins. He also held the major league record of 3,508 strikeouts. Going into the 1982 season that record had stood for 55 years. Now Nolan, with 3,249 strikeouts, had a chance. He needed 260 more and the record would be his.

The Walter Johnson record had been set 20 years before Nolan was even born. It had been a record for so long that it was thought to be unbreakable.

The 1970s had produced a bumper crop of strikeout pitchers. Even though the record had stood for so long, there were three other active pitchers—Gaylord Perry, Tom Seaver, and Steve Carlton—who also had a chance at the record. Perry was actually 87 career strike-outs ahead of Nolan, and Carlton wasn't far behind.

Nolan wanted to be the first to break the record. He knew he had to get busy.

Nolan gave Houston another good year of pitching in 1982. The Astros didn't make the playoffs but Nolan had done his part. He ended up with the most wins on the pitching staff with a 16–12 record. He also finished third in the National League in strikeouts, with 245—only 15 short of breaking Johnson's record.

Nolan wasn't usually into baseball history. But that off-season he learned about Walter Johnson. The more he learned, the more he wanted the record.

Heading into the 1983 season, Nolan had 3,494 strikeouts, Perry had 3,452, Carlton had 3,334, and Seaver had 3,137. Perry was nearing retirement; he had managed only 116 strikeouts in 1982, and was unlikely to catch Nolan. Unless Nolan was injured.

Nolan did have some minor injuries in spring training. He pitched only eighteen innings. Then he was hospitalized with an illness when the season opened. Was it possible that Perry could catch him?

Nolan was finally ready to pitch by the twelfth game of the season. He was in the Dome against Montreal. He pitched well. The Astros won the game. Nolan ended up with seven strikeouts including career number 3,500 against Andre Dawson.

Next up were the Phillies. Nolan was trying to strike out every batter. He tried too hard. He struck out only three, walked six, and lost the game.

On April 27, Nolan's next start came in Montreal against the Expos. Nolan concentrated on pitching. The strikeouts had to take care of themselves.

Nolan entered the eighth inning with only three strikeouts. He struck out Tim Blackwell for number 3,508. He was tied for the record.

Pinch-hitter Brad Mills, a lefthander, was next. He was all that stood between Nolan and the record. Nolan was determined to get his strikeout now.

Nolan checked his catcher Alan Ashby for the sign. Fastball. Nolan gripped the seams, wound up, and delivered. *Thwap!* "Strike one."

Nolan checked the sign again. Fastball. Nolan wound up and delivered. Mills swung and missed. "Strike two."

Ashby gave Nolan the sign for a fastball, outside. That was a smart call with the count 0–2. Maybe Mills would swing at a pitch he couldn't hit. Nolan wound up and delivered. *Thwap!* Right where he wanted it. Just off the outside corner. But Mills didn't swing. "Ball one."

The Expo fans had come out to Olympic Stadium that day hoping to see the Expos win and Nolan set the record. They were now cheering for Nolan against their own team.

Nolan checked the sign. Ashby wanted a fastball. Maybe in his younger days, but not today. Nolan shook him off. Ashby gave him the sign for a backdoor curve. That's a pitch that starts off outside and breaks over the plate at the last instant.

This was possibly the most important pitch of

Nolan's career. He had enough confidence in his curve-ball to use it. Just as with his fourth no-hitter, Nolan no longer had to use his fastball when he needed a big pitch.

Nolan went into his wind-up and delivered. The pitch started outside and broke just like Nolan wanted. Mills had no time to react as he watched it hit Ashby's glove. For a millisecond everyone held their breath. The home plate umpire made the call: "Strike!"

Nolan had done it. He had broken the 56-year-old record. Number 3,509 was history!

All 19,307 Expo fans were screaming. The scoreboard flashed up pictures of Nolan and Walter Johnson. Nolan stood on the mound, soaking it all in. Then he tipped his cap to the fans.

It was a fantastic record to hold. But Nolan had done it in 2,500 fewer innings than Johnson. That made it even more impressive.

Baseball records are funny. Some of them seem un-breakable and are later shattered. When Roger Maris' single-season home run record of 61 was broken, it had stood for 27 years. But when it was broken in 1998, it was broken by *both* Mark McGwire and Sammy Sosa. McGwire absolutely destroyed it by hitting 70.

It was the same with Walter Johnson's record. Later in that 1983 season, both Steve Carlton and Gaylord Perry broke it. Seaver broke it in 1986, his last season.

Perry retired in 1983, and Carlton's big strikeout

years were behind him. Nolan still had many years ahead of him. He set his sights on 4,000.

The 1983 season was another disappointing one for the Astros. They again finished out of the playoffs. Nolan finished with a 14–9 record and 183 strikeouts.

The next two seasons were tough for Nolan. The Astros were no longer contending for the pennant. Nolan had a bunch of nagging injuries. He finished with disappointing 12–11 and 10–12 records.

But 1985 was not without its highlights. On July 11, Nolan recorded strikeout number 4,000 against Danny Heep of the New York Mets. Just as he had done with Brad Mills, Nolan used a curveball to get that historic strikeout.

Nolan was rewarded by being named to his sixth All-Star team. Pete Rose had reached a milestone as well, with his 4,000th hit that season. Nolan and Pete were honored by being allowed to throw out the ceremonial first pitch.

Later, when the pitches counted, Nolan threw three scoreless innings against the American League All-Stars. He struck out two.

The Astros weren't expected to be a good ball club in 1986. But the Astros surprised everyone. Mike Scott had his best season ever as a pitcher. He won eighteen games, pitched a no-hitter, and led the league in both strikeouts and ERA.

Nolan got off to a terrible start. He was 3–6 and

pitching with pain. Finally, he went on the disabled list twice.

The pain never really went away. But Nolan finished the season strong. He won five of his last six decisions. He finished the season 12–8 with 194 strikeouts in 178 innings of pitching.

The Astros faced the Mets in the best-of-seven League Championship Series. The Astros won the first game 1–0 behind a 14-strikeout performance by Mike Scott. Nolan and the Astros lost the second game. The teams split the next two games, tying the series at 2–2.

Game 5 was in Shea Stadium. Nolan was to pitch against Dwight Gooden. The game was a sellout, and both teams desperately wanted to win.

Here was Nolan playing in the post-season on the same mound where he pitched so well in the 1969 World Series. The memories of past seasons, good and bad, came flooding back.

Nolan pitched a great game. So did Dwight Gooden. It was an old-fashioned pitchers' duel.

Nolan pitched nine complete innings. He struck out 12. He allowed just two hits and one run. A great game—but after nine innings the score was tied 1–1. Nolan was exhausted, so the decision was made to go to a relief pitcher for the 10th.

The Mets ended up winning 2–1 in the 12th. They then won the next game and the series.

The strangest season of Nolan's career was 1987.

The general manager, Dick Wagner, decided to put Nolan on a pitch count. As soon as he reached 115 pitches, he was to be taken out of the game no matter what the situation. The idea was to protect Nolan from injuries.

Nolan objected. But he finally had no choice. He had to obey the manager.

It made for a very frustrating season. If Nolan pitched poorly, he was the losing pitcher. If he pitched great, he was still taken out after 115 pitches and too often the relief pitchers would blow his lead.

When the season ended, Nolan led the league in strikeouts with 270 and had the league's lowest ERA at 2.76. But his win-loss record was 8–16. Simply terrible.

With his strikeouts and ERA, Nolan should have been 16–8 or maybe 20–8, not a pathetic 8–16. Nolan had too much pride to live with a silly idea like a 115-pitch limit. When Dick Wagner was fired, there was hope for 1988.

The 1987 season did have one highlight. It came in a September game in the Dome. Nolan struck out 16 Giants—not bad for a 40-year-old man. One of those strikeouts, Mike Aldrete, became strikeout victim number 4,500.

Nolan enjoyed pitching in 1988. The pitch limit was gone. He was ready to get back to real pitching.

On April 27, Nolan had an incredible performance. He pitched a no-hitter into the ninth inning against the Phillies. Mike Schmidt broke it up with a one-out single.

Nolan ended up leading the league in strikeouts with 228. He had a decent record at 12–11 and a respectable ERA of 3.52. He ended the season with 4,775 career strikeouts.

Then the Astros' management made a stupid decision. For the past eight years, Nolan had been renewing his contract at $1 million a year. Lots of players made more than that by then, but Nolan had never asked for a raise.

The new general manager, Bill Wood, offered Nolan a contract with a 20 percent pay *cut.* Nolan couldn't believe it. The pitch count had been awful, but this was an even worse insult.

Nolan explained that the Mets gave up on him and made what many considered the worst trade in baseball history. The Angels didn't try to re-sign him, and Buzzie Bavasi had regretted it ever since. Were the Astros going to join the Mets and Angels in foolishly giving up on Nolan? Wood said they were serious—a pay cut was the only way Nolan could stay with the Astros.

Nolan spent the next few months seeing if other teams were interested. Plenty were. And they were offering pay *raises,* not cuts.

Nolan finally decided he wanted to stay in Texas. Tom Grieve, the Rangers' general manager, had told Nolan he would be very welcome with the Arlington club. He offered a two-year deal with $1.6 million the first year—twice what Houston offered. Nolan accepted.

Nolan would have been happy to finish his career in Houston. The Astro fans had been great. But it wasn't to be.

Nolan would be 42 going into the next season. Deep down inside, Nolan knew he had another year or two inside him. With 273 wins and 4,775 strikeouts, maybe—just maybe—he could get to 300 wins and 5,000 strikeouts. No one dared imagine that some of his best years were still to come.

A Texas Ranger

11

THE TEXAS RANGERS WERE one of the worst teams in baseball. Since they moved from Washington and changed their name from the Senators in 1972, they had established a great tradition as losers.

All of this was about to change. The Rangers had been purchased by a new group of local investors led by George W. Bush. George's father, George Bush, had just been elected president of the United States. George W. was determined to continue the family's winning streak by turning the Rangers into a success.

The Rangers had a long way to go. They finished 1988 with a miserable 71–91 record, good for sixth in their division.

George W. and general manager Tom Grieve had

acted quickly. They had traded for sluggers Julio Franco and Rafael Palmeiro. Their third addition was Nolan.

The Rangers wanted Nolan for many reasons. They hoped he could put together another one or two decent seasons. They also wanted Nolan for his "star" qualities. Every strikeout Nolan pitched extended his record for career strikeouts. Nolan also had a great reputation as a clean-cut family man. These were all qualities the Rangers were looking for.

Unlike Houston, the Rangers heavily promoted their star pitcher. Above the ticket windows hung a huge banner, 20-foot by 24-foot, showing Nolan pitching.

Nolan had his fresh start. He had a team solidly behind him. Now it was up to Nolan. Could his 42-year-old body really continue to pitch in the big leagues?

The answer came quickly. Nolan pitched the opener at Arlington Stadium. He struck out eight Detroit Tigers before coming out for a relief pitcher. He didn't get a decision but pitched a good game.

Five days later, Nolan struck out 15 Milwaukee Brewers. Nolan and the Rangers won 8–1.

Less than two weeks later, Nolan was on the mound at Toronto's Sky Dome. After eight innings, Nolan was pitching a no-hitter! Nelson Liriano ended it with a triple. Still, Nolan came away with a tremendous pitching performance. He ended up with a one-hitter, striking out 12 and winning the game 4–1.

Next up was a big test of age versus youth. Nolan was going to face Roger Clemens and the Boston Red

113

Sox. Clemens was one of the hottest young pitchers in baseball. After winning the College Baseball World Series with the University of Texas in 1983, he had taken major league baseball by storm. In 1986 he struck out 20 batters in a single game to break Nolan's record of 19.

Clemens, like Nolan, was a Texan. He had played baseball in far west Houston at Spring Woods High School. Actually, his high school was about the same distance west of the Astrodome as Alvin High was south.

The match-up was set. Forty-two-year-old pitching legend Nolan Ryan versus 26-year-old, up-and-coming pitching legend Roger Clemens. The fans in Arlington Stadium were in for a treat.

For nine innings, the two aces dueled with 95 mph fastballs. Nolan struck out 11, Clemens struck out six. Nolan gave up three hits, Clemens gave up six. But when the game was over, there would be only one winner. It was Nolan—he and the Rangers won 2–1.

Clemens went on to a fantastic pitching career which continues today. He has already collected five Cy Young awards and holds many records. But at least for that one game, Nolan had gone head-to-head with an ace pitcher from the next generation, and Nolan had won.

Reid and Reese Ryan, now 17 and 13, were frequent visitors to Arlington Stadium. The Astros had discouraged them from coming to the Dome. The Rangers were just the opposite.

The boys were welcomed as bat boys both at home and away games. They took batting practice early and shagged flyballs during the team practice. Pitching coach Tom House also worked with them.

Tom was an interesting part of the Rangers' story. As a major league pitcher, he had experimented with weight training just as Nolan had. Now, as a pitching coach, he was trying to learn what would work best for his pitchers.

Tom had come up with an idea called cross-training. The idea was to improve your performance in your chosen sport by working in another sport. He had discovered that throwing a football would help a pitcher throw a baseball. It took a while for Nolan to warm up to the idea. But slowly he did.

Nolan and Tom worked on and improved the training program that Nolan and Gene Coleman had developed with the Astros. Nolan became a leading cross-trainer in sports—he used weight work and football tosses to make himself a better pitcher.

As the season went on, Nolan continued to pitch well. The Rangers were becoming a winning ball club, and the fans were getting excited.

Nolan kept racking up the strikeouts and kept flirting with no-hitters. He began June by pitching a one-hitter against Seattle. He struck out 11, including Seattle's superstar-to-be Ken Griffey, Jr. He ended June by taking a no-hitter to two outs in the eighth. He ended up winning the game.

By the end of June he was a sizzling 9–3. His

strikeout total stood at 4,911, just 89 strikeouts short of 5,000.

On July 6, Nolan was scheduled to pitch against California in Anaheim Stadium. It had been 10 years since Nolan had pitched in the ballpark he called home for those years with the Angels. How would the fans react to him?

As Nolan left the bullpen to take the mound at the beginning of the game, he got his answer. The crowd rose to its feet and applauded. Nolan was overwhelmed with emotion.

Nolan put the emotion aside when the game started. He was on fire all night long. He wound up striking out 12 Angels in a 3–0 shutout.

The Angel crowd wasn't going to put their emotions aside. After watching Nolan overwhelm their Angels, the fans again gave him a standing ovation.

Nolan's brilliant pitching was recognized when he was named to his seventh All-Star team. It was even more special to Nolan since it was also being played in Anaheim Stadium.

Nolan treated the All-Star game like a family reunion. He brought his kids. They enjoyed visiting with both the veterans and new stars.

Once the game started, Nolan got serious. He pitched two full innings, giving up one hit, no runs, and striking out three. He wound up being the winning pitcher—and the oldest pitcher to ever win an All-Star game.

Nolan went back to work after the All-Star break.

116

He pitched eight no-hit innings against Detroit in August. He lost it with a single to Dave Bergman in the ninth. But Nolan won the game 4–1. He struck out 13 Tigers. His career strikeout total stood at 4,986.

Nolan struck out eight Mariners in his next start. That put him just six strikeouts short of 5,000.

August 22 was to be the day. A crowd of 42,869 along with 200 reporters and 21 TV crews packed Arlington Stadium. The game was against the Oakland A's but the fans came to watch history—to see the first man to record 5,000 career strikeouts.

It was like a playoff game. The crowd was scooping up any available souvenir. It seemed like everyone had a camera.

On this typical August day in Arlington Stadium, the scoreboard temperature sign registered 101. But that was in the shade, a place that neither Nolan nor most of the fans were.

The fans were in the game from the beginning. Nolan wasn't going to disappoint them.

Jose Canseco struck out swinging in the first inning. Number 4,995. Dave Henderson became number 4,996, and Tony Phillips number 4,997 in the second. Rickey Henderson became number 4,998 in the third. Ron Hassey became 4,999 in the fourth.

Mark McGwire was on deck when Hassey struck out to end the fourth. While the Rangers batted in the bottom of the fourth, all McGwire could think about was how he did *not* want to be strikeout victim number 5,000.

In the top of the fifth, McGwire came to the plate with his knees shaking like a rookie. A home run was the farthest thing from his mind. A groundout, flyout, anything but a strikeout. Nolan gave him a pitch in the strike zone and he punched a single to center. Mark McGwire was not going to be number 5,000.

Rickey Henderson was next up in the fifth. Nolan got a full count on him. By this time, the crowd was going wild. Camera flashes filled the stadium on every two-strike pitch.

Nolan checked for the sign. Fastball. He gripped the ball, wound up, and delivered. The crowd cheered, cameras flashed. Henderson swung. "Foul ball!" The crowd let out a huge exhale.

The count stayed at 3–2. Nolan again got the fastball sign. He wound up and delivered. The crowd cheered, cameras flashed. Henderson swung. "Foul ball!" The fans let out another huge exhale.

Nolan again got a sign for a fastball, but the location was low and away. Nolan wound up and delivered. The crowd cheered, cameras flashed. Henderson swung. *Thwap!* "Strike three!"

This time the crowd didn't have to exhale. They just went crazy. The game was stopped. The crowd continued cheering.

Then a pre-recorded video was played on the centerfield scoreboard. It was President Bush congratulating Nolan.

Nolan finished the 1989 season with a 16–12 record. He led the league with 301 strikeouts. Batters hit a weak .187 against Nolan for the season.

As for the Rangers, they didn't win their division, but they did show that they were now a contender. They also drew more than 2,000,000 fans to the ballpark. They had turned a corner, and Nolan had been a big part of it.

Nolan finished the season with 289 career wins— just 11 short of the magical 300 that every great pitcher strives for. If Nolan could put together just one more respectable season, he could reach the 300-win milestone.

What really intrigued fans was the way Nolan was still flirting with no-hitters. Five times in 1989, he had taken a no-hitter to the very late innings. Could a 43-year-old man possibly pitch a no-hitter? The fans were already lining up to buy tickets to see.

AGELESS
SUPERSTAR

12

NOLAN THREW HIS WARM-UP pitches in the bullpen before the game. The date was June 11, 1990. The place was Oakland Coliseum. It was going to be a turning point for Nolan and he knew it.

He had begun 1990 as the hottest pitcher in baseball. He raced out to a 4–0 start. That included an incredible 16-strikeout, one-hit masterpiece he had thrown at the Chicago White Sox in late April.

But by May his back was in constant pain and his pitching went south—way south. He lost three games. Finally, he went on the disabled list for 15 days. When he came off it in early June, he got shellacked by the A's; he gave up five runs in five innings before being taken out. Now he was facing the A's again. The defending World Series Champion A's.

To make matters worse, both Ranger catchers Mike Stanley and Gene Petralli were out with injuries. John Russell, a former major leaguer who was coaching high school baseball, had been signed by the Rangers as an emergency replacement.

Ruth, Reese, and Wendy had made a last-minute decision to fly to Oakland to watch the game. Reid had to pitch in a summer league game, so he stayed in Alvin. Fourteen-year-old Reese went to the clubhouse to suit up as bat boy.

Sitting in the stands, Ruth had a very uneasy feeling. Was this going to be the end?

Nolan was thinking the same thing. So was everyone else. Would this be how it ends? Nolan still able to pitch one-hitters—but his back or some other part of his body giving out?

All of these thoughts were on Nolan's mind. But now it was time to play ball. Thirty-three thousand fans and a huge TV audience were waiting.

Julio Franco gave the Rangers a two-run lead with a homer in the top of the first. Nolan sat the first three A's down in order. So far so good.

John Russell, the emergency catcher, hit a solo homer in the second. That made the lead 3–0. Nolan sat down three straight A's in the second. He knew he had good stuff. Now if his back would just let him keep pitching.

Nolan gave up a walk to shortstop Walt Weiss in the third. Weiss was the very first baserunner for the

A's. But that was it for Oakland, as Nolan again sat them down.

By the time the Rangers were batting in the top of the fifth, Nolan's back was hurting badly. Reese knew what to do. He sat next to his dad and massaged his back. As Reese and Nolan watched, Julio Franco belted another two-run homer. Now the Rangers led 5–0.

When Nolan came out in the bottom of the fifth, the crowd began to whisper among themselves. Nolan had pitched four no-hit innings—an amazing feat for a 43-year-old man.

Nolan quickly retired three more batters. Make that *five* no-hit innings.

But as Nolan got to the dugout, Reese could see the pain in his father's eyes. He started massaging his back again. As the fans were quickly getting hot dogs and Cokes while the Rangers batted, a TV producer noticed the father-son drama in the dugout. The TV audience was soon witnessing this special event that the stadium fans couldn't see.

By the bottom of the sixth, the Oakland crowd was openly rooting for Nolan. They cheered his outs and began chanting, *"No-lan! No-lan!"*

With one out, Nolan walked third baseman Mike Gallego. Oakland had its second baserunner. But Nolan quickly retired the next two batters.

Nolan's pitching dominance continued through the seventh and eighth innings. The crowd was whipping itself into a frenzy. Nolan had 13 strikeouts and was pitching harder with each passing inning.

122

Still, the back was hurting. Between pitches, Nolan stepped off the mound and stretched. Reese kept up the massages.

Finally, it was the bottom of the ninth. First up was pinch hitter Ken Phelps. He had broken up a no-hitter with a ninth-inning home run two months earlier against Seattle's Brian Holmes. Could he do it twice?

No. Phelps went down on a swinging third strike. Nolan's 14th K of the game.

Next up, Rickey Henderson. Henderson was batting .342. Could he get some revenge for being Nolan's 5,000th strikeout victim?

Henderson and Nolan battled to a 2–2 count. On the next pitch, Henderson hit a slow grounder to short. Jeff Huson charged it and threw Henderson out at first. Two outs!

The fans were on their feet. *"No-lan! No-lan!"* echoed from every corner of the stadium.

The drama ended quickly when Willie Randolph hit a routine fly ball to right. Ruben Sierra made the catch.

Nolan had done it! He had pitched a record *sixth* no-hitter!

John Russell reached Nolan first. Then the rest of his teammates. They carried him off the field.

Nolan, 43, had become the oldest pitcher to ever pitch a no-hitter. It had been 17 years since Nolan's first no-hitter and nearly 10 years since his fifth.

Two days after the no-hitter, the doctors found a

123

stress fracture that was causing Nolan's back pain. There wasn't anything that could be done. Nolan could either rest it by retiring or pitch with pain. Nolan decided to keep pitching. It would be painful, but at least Nolan knew what the problem was.

By now Nolan was fixing his concentration on the one big milestone left—300 wins. As exciting as the sixth no-hitter was, it was also win number 294.

Nolan began a winning streak on June 22 against Seattle. He beat them in Arlington 5–2. Win number 295.

Then came Minnesota on the road. They fell 9–2. Win number 296.

Next up were the Boston Red Sox. Nolan struck out 12 as they fell 7–4. Win number 297.

A road game at Detroit was next. They fell 5–3. Win number 298.

A week later the Tigers were back in Arlington for a rematch. Nolan came out on top again. Win number 299.

Nolan's next start came in front of the home crowd at Arlington. The game was a complete sellout. It was carried on nationwide TV. All of America was waiting for Nolan to reach the 300-win mark. All of America except the New York Yankees, that is.

Deion Sanders led off with a triple. It got worse. Nolan was taken out of the game after being rocked for seven runs. The Rangers later rallied so that Nolan avoided the loss, but it was a huge disappointment to everyone.

Five days later, the scene was reset. Nolan was pitching in Milwaukee against the Brewers. Fifty-five thousand fans—standing room only—were crammed into County Stadium. The national media, 250 strong, were on hand to record history. Back in Arlington, 8,000 fans went to Arlington Stadium for a special closed-circuit telecast. Millions more were glued to TV sets.

Nolan pitched well. He mowed down the first eight Brewers in order. Then with two out in the bottom of the third, Nolan gave up a single to Paul Molitor. Robin Yount followed with a deep shot to right; it bounced off the top of the fence for an RBI triple.

The Rangers responded with a four-run rally in the top of the fifth. They added a run in the sixth to give Nolan a 5–1 lead.

With the lead, Nolan seemed to pitch better. He got five of the next nine outs on strikeouts.

Going into the bottom of the eighth, the Rangers still led 5–1. But the defense got shaky. After two fielding errors, the Brewers closed the lead to 5–3.

With two outs, Ranger manager Bobby Valentine had to make a decision. Nolan had thrown 146 pitches. It was time to bring in a reliever. But Valentine had to wonder if it was the right thing to do.

The crowd, however, knew what they wanted. When Valentine walked to the mound and took Nolan out, they let out a long, loud *"Boo!"*

But as Nolan walked to the dugout, the crowd rose to their feet. They gave him a huge standing ovation.

They had seen Nolan pitch a good game. Whether they had watched history was still to be determined.

Reliever Brad Arnsberg came in to get the last out in the eighth.

The Rangers exploded in the top of the ninth. They scored six runs—four on a Julio Franco grand slam. Arnsberg got the final three outs in the bottom of the ninth. The Rangers won. Nolan had win number 300!

Nolan joined Cy Young, Walter Johnson, Christy Mathewson, Grover Alexander, and Warren Spahn in the 300-win club. Only 19 pitchers had ever done it. Nolan was the 20th.

By now, Nolan Ryan fever swept America. He was the most talked-about superstar in sports. Everyone was his fan. Stadiums were filled when he pitched. Advertisers clamored for his endorsement. On the road, even the other teams' fans would root for Nolan.

Nolan closed the 1990 season with an 11-strikeout performance. Nolan had a miracle year. At age 43 he had posted a 13–9 record, led his league in strikeouts for the fourth consecutive year, had pitched a no-hitter, and notched his 300th career win. The excitement was already building for 1991.

Nolan's only regret for the 1990 season was that his mother had not lived to see it. She had outlived his father by 20 years, still living in the house where Nolan had grown up. Nolan made it a practice to call her every single day. One day in January there was no answer. She had died unexpectedly.

She had seen most of Nolan's career. In 1987 she had flown to Williamsport, Pennsylvania, where she was honored as Little League "Mother of the Year." She had also been active in her grandchildren's lives. As Reid would say, "Grandma Ryan was our home base."

Before the 1991 season, a special exhibition game was scheduled. The Rangers were going to play a college team—the University of Texas—at Disch–Falk Field in Austin. Nolan would be the starting pitcher for the Rangers. The University of Texas was going to start a little used freshman pitcher named Reid Ryan.

Ryan v. Ryan was a matchup made in media heaven. The press and the public loved it.

Of course, there was a risk the game would be a farce. Reid would be overmatched by a heavy-hitting Ranger line-up. Nolan would be in less than top form going against college players who would be hungry for a career highlight with a hit off a legend.

Still the match-up offered something special—a special quality that had made baseball America's pastime. Baseball was a game that was passed from generation to generation. A father would teach his son to play catch and take him to his first professional game. Twenty years later, the son would do the same for his son or daughter and the tradition would continue. A father-son pitching match-up was simply irresistible.

America had fallen in love with Nolan. Not just Nolan the man, but Nolan the image.

In a professional sports world where police reports and drug rehab programs seemed as important as home runs and strikeouts, Nolan was the All-American favorite. He represented hard work, perseverance, and family values. It was the Good Guy v. The Bad Boys. Nolan's success was proof that the good guys were winning.

The Ryan v. Ryan match-up turned out just fine. Ruth, mother and wife of the pitchers, threw out the first pitch. Reid took on the Rangers' sluggers for two innings, gave up four runs, but had a decent showing. Nolan went three innings, giving up a couple of hits and a run. The college players and fans left with an unforgettable memory. And America enjoyed every bit of it.

It was a month later that Nolan was preparing to pitch at Arlington Stadium against the Toronto Blue Jays. Everything hurt. His back was sore. His Achilles tendon was sore. Some scar tissue on one of the fingers on his pitching hand tore open during warm-ups. He warned Tom House, his pitching coach, that he wouldn't last long. "I feel old today, Tom," said Nolan.

Nolan retired the first two Blue Jays he faced in the first inning. Heavy-hitting Kelly Gruber was next. Nolan took him to 3–2, but walked him on the next pitch. Nolan got leftfielder Joe Carter to hit into an out to end the first.

In the second, first baseman Jon Olerud led off. Nolan got two strikes on him. Catcher Mike Stanley signaled for a curve. Nolan came in with a sharp breaking pitch. "Strike three!"

Next was rightfielder Mark Whiten. Nolan again got two strikes on him. Stanley called for a curveball. Nolan delivered it perfectly. "Strike three!"

Designated-hitter Glenallen Hill was next. Nolan went to a two-strike count. Stanley wanted another curve. Nolan delivered. "Strike three!"

Nolan had struck out the side. More importantly, he knew his curveball was unhittable and his fastball was going exactly where he wanted it. If his body could just hold out, he knew he could pitch another great game.

Ruben Sierra hit a two-run homer in the bottom of the third. The Rangers added one more run to lead 3–0.

With a three-run lead, Nolan came out and sat the Blue Jays down in order in the fourth. Same in the fifth. In the sixth, shortstop Manny Lee hit a bloop fly to shallow center. Gary Pettis, a five-time Gold Glove winner, took off fast and caught it at his knees. Nolan finished the Blue Jays off in the sixth.

In the seventh, Nolan walked Joe Carter on another 3–2 pitch. But Carter stayed on first as Nolan got the rest of the outs.

By the eighth inning, Arlington Stadium was electrified. Fans were driving from all over Dallas and Fort Worth to get to the game. ESPN, which was showing the Detroit–Kansas City game, decided to switch to Arlington for the final two innings. Word spread throughout America as fans interrupted what they were doing to find a TV set.

Nolan got Mark Whiten to hit into an out. One down.

Glenallen Hill was next. He became Nolan's fourteenth strikeout victim of the game. Two down.

Greg Myers was next. He was strikeout victim 15. Three down. Nolan had a no-hitter through the eighth.

Nolan had lost no-hitters in the ninth inning before. But there was something very special going on tonight. Nolan's fastball was screaming in at 96 mph right where he wanted it. His curveball was breaking hard; it was unhittable. His change-up worked whenever he needed it. At 44 years old, Nolan was pitching one of the most dominating games of his career.

The crowd at Arlington Stadium continued to grow. The ESPN audience grew. The fans in Kansas City were ignoring the live game in front of them to watch the Rangers–Toronto game being shown on the scoreboard.

The crowd launched into the now familiar *"No-lan! No-lan!"* chant as Nolan took the mound for the ninth.

First up was Manny Lee. He hit a routine grounder. One out!

Next came Devon White. Another routine grounder. Two outs!

Roberto Alomar was next. Roberto's father Sandy had been the Angels' second baseman when Nolan pitched his first no-hitter. Nolan had watched Roberto grow up and had given him baseball tips when he was a kid.

Nolan put all that out of his head. All that mattered was one batter stood between Nolan and his seventh no-hitter.

130

Nolan battled Roberto. The count went to 2–2. The fans were going crazy on every pitch.

Nolan delivered the 2–2 pitch. Roberto swung. "Strike three!" Nolan had his *seventh* no-hitter!

The stadium broke into pandemonium. The fans were screaming! Nolan threw his arm in the air. His teammates carried him off the field on their shoulders. They stopped the game in Kansas City as the fans rose and gave Nolan a standing ovation.

Nolan finished the season with a 12–6 record. His ERA of 2.91 was fifth best in the league. At 44, he had put together his third straight good season.

Looking back on those first three seasons with the Rangers, it was truly an amazing run. He had been given up on by the Mets, Angels, and Astros. Ten years earlier he had been written off as a pitcher who could only go seven innings, a pitcher at the end of his career.

But Nolan had shown everyone—himself included. In three years he had achieved his 5,000th strikeout and his 300th win, pitched his sixth and seventh no-hitters, twice led the league in strikeouts, and compiled an amazing 41–25 record. Only his first three years with the Angels, when he was still in his twenties, could compare.

There was only one question left: When would it end?

FAREWELL

THE ASTRODOME WAS crammed with 53,657 fans—the largest crowd to ever see a professional baseball game in Texas. But they were there for something else besides a game. It was a farewell party.

Drayton McLane, the new owner of the Astros, had invited Nolan and the Rangers to play a special exhibition game. Bitter feelings had built up between the Astros' fans and the old owners over Nolan's departure. McLane had revitalized the Astros' organization with a fan-friendly attitude that extended from the hot dog vendors to the players. He saw this game as a chance for the old wounds to heal and for the fans to give Nolan a proper goodbye.

Some 3,000 of Nolan's family and friends were in the Dome that night. Jim Watson, his high school coach, was there. So was Red Murff, who believed in Nolan when no one else did. Aubrey Horney, Nolan's high school basketball coach and Ruth's tennis coach, was there too.

During warm-up tosses, Nolan spotted another familiar face in the crowd. It was Melba Passmore, who had taught him in fifth grade. She was now 81. Nolan stopped and walked over to the stands to say hello. He gave her the ball he'd been warming up with.

It was that kind of night. Former President George Bush threw out the first pitch. The president was not only a good friend of Nolan's, but he was an ardent baseball fan too. At Yale, Bush had played on a team that went to the College World Series. Now that he was out of the White House, Bush was a frequent visitor to Astros' games.

Nolan had announced earlier that 1993 would be his last season in baseball. The 1992 season had been a tough one on him. He had been plagued by nagging injuries. He did manage to start 27 games but pitched just 157 innings—his lowest number in a full season since his days with the Mets. There were flashes of brilliance in his pitching that year. In July he had struck out 13 Yankees in a 4–1 victory. But his final record for the season was 5–9, with only 146 strikeouts.

Nolan talked it over with his family. First with Ruth, then with Reid, Reese, and Wendy. They all knew

133

that at age 46, his 27th season would have to be his last.

The Rangers' home opener came against the Boston Red Sox. Nolan was on the mound. He pitched the Rangers to a 3–1 victory, striking out five along the way.

Any thoughts of Nolan having a solid final season, however, were soon dashed. He had to have knee surgery later that month. Before he recovered from that surgery, he pulled a hip muscle. While rehabilitating that muscle, he cut his foot.

He spent a total of 73 days on the disabled list. Still, in typical Nolan Ryan fashion, he came back in July to pitch the Rangers to a 5–3 victory over the Brewers. By August he was back on the disabled list.

The Rangers' big tribute to Nolan came on September 12. The stadium was packed with 40,000 fans. But some of those fans were special.

Hall of Famer Sandy Koufax, one of Nolan's boyhood idols, was there. So were six of the catchers that caught his no-hitters and a bunch of other former teammates.

But not just friends and teammates were there. Former opponents came too. Four of his most important strikeout victims came. Brad Mills, whose strikeout broke the Walter Johnson record, was there. So were Ron LeFlore, career strikeout number 2,000, Cesar Geronimo, number 3,000, and Danny Heep, 4,000.

By September 22, Nolan had been back pitching for a month. He had a 5–4 record and was hoping for a couple of decent games to finish off his career.

Nolan was pitching against Seattle in the King Dome. A crowd of 40,000 was on hand to get one last glimpse of a pitching legend.

Nolan couldn't get anyone out. He was in pain on every pitch. With the bases loaded, Dann Howitt hit a grand slam.

The next two batters got on. Dave Magaden came to the plate. Nolan got behind in the count 2–0.

Nolan took a deep breath. He put his foot to the rubber and looked at his catcher for the sign. Fastball.

Nolan checked the runners. He went through his stretch motion and delivered.

The pain was instant. His elbow popped. Nolan's right arm fell limp to his side. After 27 seasons, Nolan had thrown his last pitch.

Perhaps it was unfair for Nolan to pitch his last game this way. He deserved better. He deserved to go out with one final swinging "Strike three."

Still, this was the way Nolan had to go out. He loved baseball; he loved the fans. He pitched until he couldn't pitch anymore. He went out throwing one last fastball.

But the official career of a baseball legend doesn't end on the playing field. There is a five-year waiting period, then one final stop. It is in a small New York village called Cooperstown.

COOPERSTOWN

1994–1999

THE VILLAGE OF COOPERSTOWN is set at the base of Otsego Lake in the rolling hills of upstate New York. Farmland, dotted with red barns, surrounds it.

The village itself, home to around 2,500 people, has lots of frame houses with neatly maintained lawns and flower gardens. Trees line the streets. Main Street, with a downtown of two or so blocks, has red brick buildings from one end to the other.

Cooperstown is like a picture postcard. There are no fast food restaurants or bright neon signs. In fact, Cooperstown today looks much as it did back in 1939, when the Baseball Hall of Fame opened there.

But Cooperstown is much more than a village in New York. The very name stands for excellence. Not one-season, flash-in-the-pan type excellence but a whole career of excellence. The kind of career that is marked by 3,000 hits or 500 homers or 300 wins. Babe Ruth, Cy Young, Willie Mays, and Hank Aaron type careers.

The first five legends elected to the Hall—Ty Cobb, Babe Ruth, Honus Wagner, Christy Mathewson, and Walter Johnson—set the standard of career excellence for the others to follow. Cobb played for 24 seasons as he amassed 4,191 hits. Ruth launched 714 homers over a spectacular 22-season career. Wagner played flawlessly at shortstop as he put together 17 straight seasons where his batting average topped .300. Mathewson kept batters off balance with his fadeaway pitch for 17 seasons as he won 373 games. Johnson's sweeping sidearm fastball terrorized batters for 21 years as he struck out 3,508 while winning an amazing 416 games.

These first five legends were elected in 1936. By the time the Hall of Fame building opened in 1939, Cy Young, Lou Gehrig, Grover Cleveland Alexander, and 17 other immortals from baseball's early years joined the original five members.

Baseball writers, who vote on membership, hold annual elections to select deserving players. The ranks of the original 25 have grown to 201 players as baseball's very best are added. Their numbers increase, even though Hall of Fame standards have remained high.

July 25, 1999, was the day set for Nolan to join the ranks of baseball's legends. His career of excellence had led the baseball writers to give him the second highest vote total in Hall of Fame history.

Induction day began early for the Ryan family. Nolan, Ruth, Reid, Reese, and Wendy had rooms at the Otesaga Resort—some of the very few rooms available in Cooperstown. Their first official activity was a lavish brunch held by the Texas Rangers on the grounds of the Fenimore Museum. Current Rangers owner Tom Hicks and former Rangers owner, now Texas governor, George W. Bush were there. So were about 150 Ryan family and friends. It was a time to remember for those who knew him as a boy in Alvin and those who met him along the way.

That was Nolan's last chance with his family and closest friends. He was soon swept off to the main event—the induction ceremony.

Some 50,000 fans had flooded into Cooperstown. Main Street, where the actual Hall of Fame is located, was too small for that crowd. Instead, the ceremony was held on a grassy field outside of town at the Clark Sports Center.

The crowd, along with a live ESPN audience, witnessed a very special ceremony. Two other baseball legends, George Brett and Robin Yount, were also being added to the immortals that day. Brett had a spectacular 21-season career with the Kansas City Royals that included 3,154 hits, while Yount had spent his 20 seasons piling up 3,142 hits with the Milwaukee Brewers.

Thirty-four Hall of Fame legends took the stage. Among them were Ted Williams and Stan Musial, Willie

Mays and Hank Aaron, Tom Seaver and Reggie Jackson—three generations of the greatest living legends of baseball. But the front row was reserved for the newest legends—Ryan, Brett, and Yount.

As Nolan looked out at the sea of fans, he spotted his family. Ruth with her hand on Reid's arm, followed by Wendy and Reese. His brother and four sisters were there too.

Nolan couldn't help but think back to Alvin—to remember when he was a nine-year-old boy on a team called the Rangers. Now, 43 years later, his career finally was ending again as a Ranger. There had been so many teams and uniforms and players and pitches in between. It all came rushing back as he sat there.

Finally, his moment came. Baseball Commissioner Bud Selig began to speak into the microphone. Nolan walked over and stood next to him.

As the plaque was unveiled, Selig began to read: "A fierce competitor . . . overwhelming fastball." Then came the numbers: 324 wins, 5,714 strikeouts, 7 no-hitters, 12 one-hitters, 6 seasons with over 300 strikeouts, 383 strikeouts in one season. The plaque said it all.

Now it was Nolan's turn to speak. "My ability to throw a baseball was a gift. It was a God-given gift," he explained. "I had the pleasure . . . to live a childhood dream . . . to play youth baseball."

Nolan acknowledged his wife and children. He recognized Glenn York, Aubrey Horner, and Jim Watson, his coaches from junior high and high school.

Then he began thanking the dozens of people who had helped his career. As Nolan knew, if Red Murff hadn't believed in him he probably never would have been in the majors. Nolan knew about the rocky start with the Mets and how Ruth had talked him into sticking with baseball. He also remembered how Tom Morgan and Jeff Torborg had worked with him in his first season with the Angels to turn him from a raw talent to a polished professional. And he knew that Gene Coleman and Tom House, along with all that conditioning work, had allowed him to pitch long after most players retired. He thanked them all.

It was time for Nolan to finish. He looked at the 50,000 faces in front of him and made one last thank you. This one was for the fans. "I was truly blessed by the fans . . . I may be gone, but I won't forget you. And I appreciate all those times that you supported me over the 27 years."

Nolan's official baseball career came to an end. He was now a Hall of Famer.

Today Nolan and Ruth still live in Alvin. He remains active as a businessman, rancher, and volunteer commissioner on the Texas Parks and Wildlife Board. He does product endorsements for companies like Southwest Airlines and Dairy Queen, and he still works for the Texas Rangers baseball team.

One of Nolan's current businesses is his part ownership of a double-A minor league team scheduled to open the 2000 season in Round Rock, Texas. His son Reid is the team president. To Nolan's delight, their new stadium is located within view of the baseball complex for Round Rock's youth baseball programs.

Who knows what future star or even Hall of Famer may play on his double-A team or be a youth player on the nearby field? How many young players will be inspired by Nolan's career, just as Nolan was by Hank Aaron, Roberto Clemente, and Sandy Koufax?

That is exactly why baseball is America's game. Not because of the crack of a bat, a thrilling double play, a hot dog at the stadium, or all the records and big league stars. No, baseball is our game because it is passed from generation to generation.

Baseball began as something called "Town Ball" back when the United States was a new country with a president named Washington and a new idea called democracy. Since then our country has fought a Civil War and two World Wars. We have moved from a nation of farmers to the industrial age to the beginning of a technology age. Through all these changes, baseball has remained constant. There has always been a boy who needed to learn to play catch. There was a father who showed him how to hit a ball—and to run to first not third. There was always a story to tell about how a grandfather had seen a legend play.

The Hall of Fame has one huge room where all the players' plaques are hung in a gallery. One of the last three plaques in that Hall of Fame gallery belongs to Nolan Ryan. Nolan was the best fastball pitcher of his

141

day. He broke Walter Johnson's career strikeout record and set a new "unbreakable" career strikeout record of 5,714.

But no record is truly "unbreakable." Somewhere, someplace, there is a kid who has to be taught which hand to put the glove on and how to throw the ball. There is a kid who will have to play his first youth league game and play on through high school. The kid will have to be discovered by a scout, have to survive the rocky times, have to have coaches to help, and have to work very hard. That kid will do just what Nolan Ryan did. He will break an unbreakable record and take his place in Cooperstown.

What really makes baseball special is that that kid could be you.

NOLAN RYAN
TIMELINE

1947   Born January 31, at Refugio, Texas; family moves
        to Alvin six weeks later.
1965   Pitches Alvin High School to State Championship
        game; drafted by New York Mets as 295th pick.
1966   Records 17–2 record for single-A Greenville; pitch-
        es three innings in majors for Mets.
1967   Marries Ruth in Alvin on June 22.
1968   Joins Mets as a regular; military duty limits appear-
        ances.
1969   Pitches in World Series, which Mets win.
1971   Son, Robert Reid, born November 21; traded to
        California Angels.
1973   Pitches no-hitters No. 1 and No. 2 against Kansas
        City on May 15 and Detroit on July 15; sets single-
        season strikeout record.
1974   Pitches no-hitter No. 3 against Minnesota on
        September 28.

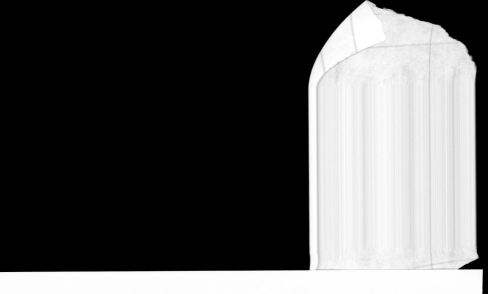

1975	Pitches no-hitter No. 4 against Baltimore on June 1.
1976	Son, Nolan Reese, born on January 21.
1977	Daughter, Wendy Lynn, born on March 22.
1979	After season signs as free agent for $1 million with Houston Astros, making him highest paid player in team sports.
1981	Pitches no-hitter No. 5 against Los Angeles on September 26.
1983	Breaks Walter Johnson's career strikeout record, with 3,509.
1989	Signs as free agent with Texas Rangers; records strikeout number 5,000 on August 22.
1990	Pitches no-hitter No. 6 versus Oakland on June 11; wins career victory 300 on July 31.
1991	Pitches no-hitter No. 7 against Toronto on May 1.
1993	Pitches last game on September 22 when arm injury forces him out.
1999	Inducted into Hall of Fame on July 25.

NOLAN RYAN
RECORDS

Hall of Fame Votes
(percent of ballots)

Tom Seaver	98.84%
Nolan Ryan	98.79%
Ty Cobb	98.23%
George Brett	98.19%
Hank Aaron	97.83%
Mike Schmidt	96.52%
Johnny Bench	96.42%
Steve Carlton	95.82%
Babe Ruth	95.13%
Honus Wagner	95.13%

Single-Season Strikeouts

1.	Nolan Ryan (1973)	383
2.	Sandy Koufax (1965)	382
3.	Nolan Ryan (1974)	367
4.	Rube Waddell (1904)	349
5.	Bob Feller (1946)	348
6.	Nolan Ryan (1977)	341
7.	Nolan Ryan (1972)	329
8.	Nolan Ryan (1976)	327
9.	Sam McDowell (1965)	325
10.	Curt Schilling (1997)	319

145

Career Strikeouts

1. Nolan Ryan   5,714
2. Steve Carlton   4,136
3. Bert Blyleven   3,701
4. Tom Seaver   3,640
5. Don Sutton   3,574
6. Gaylord Perry   3,534
7. Walter Johnson   3,508
8. Phil Niekro   3,342
9. Ferguson Jenkins   3,192
10. Roger Clemens   3,153
    (thru 1998)

Shutout Games

1. Walter Johnson   110
2. Grover Alexander   90
3. Christy Mathewson   83
4. Cy Young   76
5. Eddie Plank   64
6. Warren Spahn   63
7. Nolan Ryan   61
7. Tom Seaver   61
9. Bert Blyleven   60
10. Ed Walsh   58
10. Don Sutton   58

Strikeout Milestones

No.	Date	Batter	Team
1	Sept. 11, 1966	Pat Jarvis	Braves
1,000	July 3, 1973	Sal Bando	A's
1,500	August 25, 1974	Sandy Alomar	Yankees
2,000	August 31, 1976	Ron LeFlore	Tigers
2,500	August 12, 1978	Buddy Bell	Indians
3,000	July 4, 1980	Cesar Geronimo	Reds
3,500	April 17, 1983	Andre Dawson	Expos
3,509	April 27, 1983	Brad Mills	Expos
4,000	July 11, 1985	Danny Heep	Mets
4,500	Sept. 9, 1987	Mike Aldrete	Giants
5,000	August 22, 1989	Rickey Henderson	A's
5,500	Sept. 30, 1991	Tino Martinez	Mariners
5,714	Sept. 17, 1993	Greg Myers	Angels

Major League Statistics

Year	Team	G	CG	IP	K	ERA	W-L
1966	Mets	2	0	3.0	6	15.00	0-1
1968	Mets	21	3	134.0	133	3.09	6-9
1969	Mets	25	2	89.1	92	3.53	6-3
1970	Mets	27	5	131.2	125	3.42	7-11
1971	Mets	30	3	152.0	137	3.97	10-14
1972	Angels	39	20	284.0	329	2.28	19-16
1973	Angels	41	26	326.0	383	2.87	21-16
1974	Angels	42	26	333.0	367	2.89	22-16
1975	Angels	28	10	198.0	186	3.45	14-12
1976	Angels	39	21	284.0	327	3.36	17-18
1977	Angels	37	22	299.0	341	2.77	19-16
1978	Angels	31	14	235.0	260	3.71	10-13
1979	Angels	34	17	223.0	223	3.59	16-14
1980	Astros	35	4	234.0	200	3.35	11-10
1981	Astros	21	5	149.0	140	1.69	11-5
1982	Astros	35	10	250.1	245	3.16	16-12
1983	Astros	29	5	196.1	183	2.98	14-9
1984	Astros	30	5	183.2	197	3.04	12-11
1985	Astros	35	4	232.0	209	3.80	10-12
1986	Astros	30	1	178.0	194	3.34	12-8
1987	Astros	34	0	211.2	270	2.76	8-16
1988	Astros	33	4	220.0	228	3.52	12-11
1989	Rangers	32	6	239.1	301	3.20	16-10
1990	Rangers	30	5	204.0	232	3.44	13-9
1991	Rangers	27	2	173.0	203	2.91	12-6
1992	Rangers	27	2	157.1	157	3.72	5-9
1993	Rangers	13	0	66.1	46	4.88	5-5
Career		**807**	**222**	**5,386.0**	**5,714**	**3.19**	**324-292**

147

G	=	games
CG	=	complete games
IP	=	innings pitched
K	=	strikeouts
ERA	=	earned run average
W-L	=	wins, losses

No-Hitters

Number 1
May 15, 1973
Angels 3, Royals 0

Angels	IP	H	R	ER	BB	K
Ryan (W 5-3)	9	0	0	0	3	12

Number 2
July 15, 1973
Angels 6, Tigers 0

Angels	IP	H	R	ER	BB	K
Ryan (W 11-11)	9	0	0	0	4	17

Number 3
September 28, 1974
Angels 4, Twins 0

Angels	IP	H	R	ER	BB	K
Ryan (W 22-16)	9	0	0	0	8	15

Number 4
June 1, 1975
Angels 1, Orioles 0

Angels	IP	H	R	ER	BB	K
Ryan (W 9-3)	9	0	0	0	4	9

Number 5
September 26, 1981
Astros 5, Dodgers 0

Angels	IP	H	R	ER	BB	K
Ryan (W 10-5)	9	0	0	0	3	11

Number 6
June 11, 1990
Rangers 5, A's 0

Rangers	IP	H	R	ER	BB	K
Ryan (W 5-3)	9	0	0	0	2	14

Number 7
May 1, 1991
Rangers 3, Toronto 0

Rangers	IP	H	R	ER	BB	K
Ryan (W 3-2)	5	0	0	0	2	16

IP = innings pitched
H = hits allowed
R = runs
ER = earned runs
BB = walks
K = strikeouts

Strikeout Victims

Hall of Fame Hitters

Hank Aaron (4)
Ernie Banks (3)
Johnny Bench (7)
George Brett (18)
Lou Brock (8)
Rod Carew (29)
Roberto Clemente (6)
Reggie Jackson (22)
Al Kaline (3)
Harmon Killebrew (11)

Eddie Mathews (1)
Willie McCovey (1)
Joe Morgan (6)
Brooks Robinson (8)
Mike Schmidt (15)
Willie Stargell (8)
Carl Yastrzemski (7)
Robin Yount (16)

All-Star Hitters

Albert Belle (5)
Wade Boggs (6)
Barry Bonds (3)
Jose Canseco (8)
Will Clark (12)
Andrew Dawson (26)
Cecil Fielder (4)
Carlton Fisk (24)
Ken Griffey, Jr. (5)
Tony Gwynn (9)
Ricky Henderson (5)
Bo Jackson (12)
Chuck Knoblauch (4)
Barry Larkin (1)

Roger Maris (2)
Mark McGwire (6)
Paul Molitor (12)
Rafael Palmeiro (2)
Kirby Puckett (8)
Cal Ripken, Jr. (4)
Pete Rose (13)
Ryne Sandberg (11)
Deion Sanders (3)
Darryl Strawberry (15)
Frank Thomas (11)
Mo Vaughn (2)
Dave Winfield (8)

Places to Visit

Nolan Ryan Exhibit. Alvin, Texas. Located on campus of Alvin Community College at 2925 South Bypass 35. State of the art exhibits, videos of his playing days, 17-minute film of his early life. Highlight is interactive exhibit where you can be Nolan's catcher and hear and feel his fastball hit your mitt. A must for every Nolan Ryan fan. (281) 388-1134.

Baseball Hall of Fame and Museum. Cooperstown, New York. Located at 25 Main Street downtown. The exhibits and multi-media make the history of baseball come alive. Grandstand Theater show isn't to be missed. Plaques in gallery of baseball's greatest legends. (888) 425-5633/ www.baseballhalloffame.org.

Legends of the Game Baseball Museum and Learning Center. Arlington, Texas. Located at the Ballpark in Arlington. Boasts the largest collection of baseball memorabilia outside of Cooperstown. Loads of exhibits plus a first-class interactive kids center. (817) 273-5600.

Figure Your Own Stats

Have you ever wanted to figure your own batting average or ERA? It's simple. There is just a rule to follow and then basic division or multiplication.

151

How to Figure Your Own Batting Average

Rule: Divide the number of hits by the number of times you batted. Don't include walks or sacrifices in the number of times you batted.
Example: You batted 25 times and had 9 hits.

$$
\begin{array}{r}
.360 \\
25\overline{)9.000} \\
\underline{75} \\
150 \\
\underline{150} \\
00
\end{array}
$$

Your Batting Average: .360

How to Figure Your Own Earned Run Average

Rule: Multiply all the earned runs you have given up by 9, then divide by the total number of innings you have pitched.
Example: You pitched 27 innings and gave up 10 earned runs.

$$
\begin{array}{cc}
& 3.33 \\
10 & 27\overline{)90.00} \\
\underline{\times\,9} & \underline{81} \\
90 & 90 \\
& \underline{81} \\
& 90 \\
& \underline{81}
\end{array}
$$

Your ERA: 3.33

GLOSSARY

ace—the best pitcher on the team.

All-Star Game—Held in July, this is a game between the stars of the American League and the stars of the National League. The starting players are picked by a vote of the fans. Pitchers are picked by the team manager.

American League—one of two leagues that make up major league baseball. The winning team from the American League meets the winning team from the National League in the World Series.

batting average—a number that tells the percentage of time you come to bat that you get a hit. The higher the number, the better a hitter you are. A batting average of .250 means you get one hit every four times at bat.

bullpen—an area outside of the playing field where the pitchers warm-up. It has a practice mound and plate.

change-up (or change)—a pitch that is delivered just like a fastball but is slower. It is used to fool hitters.

chase a pitch—to swing at a pitch outside the strike zone that can't be hit.

clean-up hitter—the fourth hitter in the batting order; usually the team's best power hitter.

complete game—pitcher starts and finishes the game.

corner—outside edge of home plate.

count—number of balls and strikes; balls are always listed first and a zero is read as "oh." A count of 0—2 means no balls and two strikes.

curveball—a pitch that spins and curves just as it gets to the plate.

decision—whether a pitcher wins or loses the game.

earned run—run scored without the help of an error.

ERA, Earned Run Average—average number of earned runs a pitcher gives up over nine innings. An ERA of 3.00 means the pitcher gives up an average of 3 runs for every nine innings he pitches.

error—a messed-up play; when a fielder doesn't field a ball that he should have or makes a bad throw.

expansion team—a newly created team.

flash a sign—when the catcher gives a signal to a pitcher that tells him what kind of pitch to throw next.

free agent—when a player's contract ends he can sign to play with any other team in baseball.

full count—three balls and two strikes.

general manager—works for the team's owner; decides about trades and contracts for players.

Hall of Fame—greatest honor for a professional baseball player. Players must be retired five years before they can be elected to this honor.

heat—a really good, hard fastball.

K—strikeout.

loss—given to the pitcher for the losing team who allowed the run that put the winning team ahead to stay.

Major Leagues—the top pro leagues made up of two parts, the American League and National League.

manager—the person who runs the team on the field. He wears a uniform and works for an owner and a general manager.

National League—one of the two leagues (the American League is the other) that makes up major league baseball.

no decision—when the starting pitcher isn't given either a win or loss.

no-hitter—when a pitcher goes the entire game without allowing a hit by the other team. The other team may have some baserunners get on by walks or errors.

pennant—league championship.

RBI, Run Batted In—given to a batter when he gets a hit, walk, or sacrifice that causes his team to score a run.

save—given to a relief pitcher for the winning team if he pitches well and keeps his team in the lead.

scoring position—runners on second or third base.

scout—a baseball team's employee who looks for talented young ballplayers to sign up for the team.

shutout—a game where the pitcher does not allow any runs to score.

signal—catcher's hand sign to tell the pitcher what type of pitch to throw next.

strike out looking—batter doesn't swing at pitch but umpire calls pitch a third strike.

strike out swinging—batter swings and misses a third strike.

strike out the side—pitcher strikes out all three batters in an inning.

win—given to the pitcher for the winning team if he is pitching when his team scores the run that puts them ahead to stay.

World Series—major league baseball's championship played between the winner of the American League and National League.

BIBLIOGRAPHY

Books:
Bench, Johnny. *Baseball.* New York: Alpha Books, 1999.
Murff, Red. *The Scout.* Dallas: Word Publishing, 1996.
Ryan, Nolan. *Throwing Heat.* New York: Avon Books, 1988.
————. *Miracle Man.* Dallas: Word Publishing, 1992.
Ryan, Nolan, and Mickey Herskowitz. *Kings of the Hill.* New York: Harper Collins, 1992.
Ryan, Nolan, and Tom House. *Nolan Ryan's Pitcher's Bible.* New York: Simon and Schuster, Fireside, 1991.
Ryan, Ruth. *Covering Home: My Life with Nolan Ryan.* Dallas: Word Publishing, 1995.
Ward, Geoffrey, and Ken Burns. *Baseball: An Illustrated History.* New York: Alfred A. Knopf, 1994.

Newspapers:
Alvin Sun (various dates 1964-65).
Austin American (various dates 1965).
Dallas Morning News (various dates 1999).
Houston Chronicle (various dates 1965-99).
Houston Post (various dates 1965-__).

Other Sources:
Interviews with Nolan Ryan, February 26, 1999, and March 1, 1999.
Ryan Exhibit, Alvin Community College, Alvin, Texas.
Ryan File and Exhibits, National Baseball Hall of Fame and Library, Cooperstown, New York.

About the Author

Ken Anderson has been a baseball fan since his earliest memories. As a third-grader in Oakmont, Pennsylvania, his teacher let him listen to a radio in the back of the classroom while the hometown Pittsburgh Pirates played in the seventh game of the World Series. The deal was that Ken had to report the score each inning and had to make up all the day's work for homework. When Pirate second baseman Bill Mazeroski won the game with a ninth-inning homer, his teacher couldn't contain her excitement. She looked right at Ken and said, "No homework!"

Today Ken is the district attorney of Williamson County, Texas. Most of his days are spent dealing with murderers, robbers, or drug dealers.

Ken never forgot how important his first little league coach, teachers, parents and other adults were to him when he was growing up. So he makes sure to spend lots of time in schools talking with kids about drugs and alcohol. He also teaches Sunday school, started a special center for kids who are crime victims, and has coached many youth baseball teams.

Setting goals, working hard, and staying away from drugs are the things Ken talks to kids about. Nolan Ryan's life is one of the best examples of how hard work can really pay off. That's why Ken wanted to share the story of Nolan Ryan with you.

Another book by Ken Anderson:
You Can't Do That, Dan Moody!
The Klan-Fighting Governor of Texas
(Eakin Press)

Featured on C-SPAN's Book TV